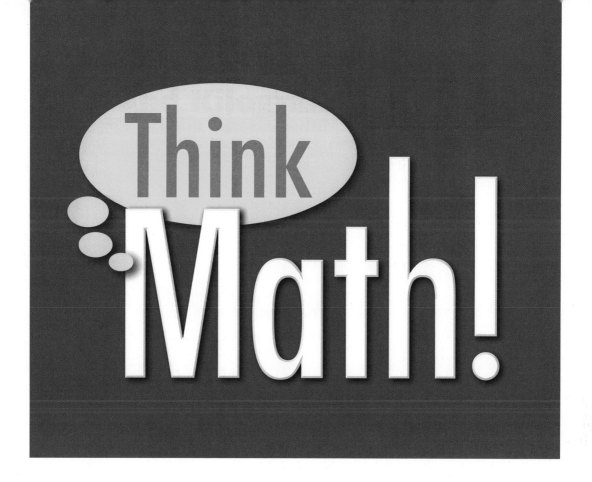

Student Handbook

Developed by Education Development Center, Inc.
through National Science Foundation

Grant No. ESI-0099093

EDC

Published and distributed by:

www.Math.SchoolSpecialty.com

Think Math! Student Handbook

Printing 5 – 6/2010

Worldcolor, Dubuque, IA

1358083

978-0-15-342476-2

This program was funded in part through the National Science Foundation under Grant No. ESI-0099093. Any opinions, findings, and conclusions or recommendations expressed in this program are those of the authors and do not necessarily reflect the views of the National Science Foundation.

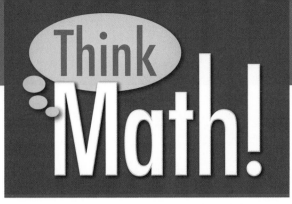

Chapter 1

Magic Squares

Chapter 2

Multiplication

Chapter 3

The Eraser Store

Chapter 4

Classifying Angles and Figures

Chapter 5

Area and Perimeter

Chapter 6

Multi-Digit Multiplication

Chapter 7

Fractions

Chapter 8 ▨

Decimals

Chapter 9 ▨

Measurement

Chapter 10

Data and Probability

Chapter 11

Three-Dimensional Geometry

Chapter 12

Extending the Number Line

Chapter 13

Division

Chapter 14

Algebraic Thinking

Chapter 15

Estimation

Chapter

1 Magic Squares

Dear Student,

As you can tell from the title of this chapter, "Magic Squares," you are about to spend some time exploring magic squares. Have you seen this type of math puzzle before?

A magic square is a grid of numbers arranged in a special way. What do you get if you add up the three numbers that make up the top row of the grid? Now try the same thing with the second row and the third row. Find the sums of the numbers in each column and each diagonal. What do you notice? Can you guess the special rule that makes this a magic square?

In this chapter, you'll use what you already know about addition, subtraction, multiplication, and division to solve puzzles and discover some interesting things about magic squares.

Mathematically yours,
The authors of
Think Math!

2	7	6
9	5	1
4	3	8

Tree Tales

There are an enormous number of trees in the world. The tallest and most massive trees are California sequoia. Some are more than 300 feet tall. The largest is so wide that it might take 25 children holding hands to circle it completely! Most trees are much smaller. Many people plant small flowering trees around their homes.

FACT·ACTIVITY 1

Larry the landscaper wants to plant groups of small flowering trees in a triangular pattern. The number of trees at the corners are shown. How many trees should he plant along each side so there are 10 trees along each line of the triangle?

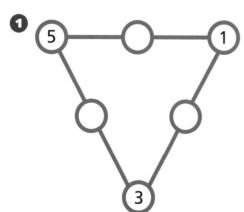

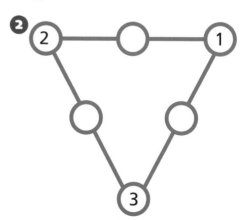

In an effort to improve the environment, a fourth grade class helps a park ranger plant a total of **136** seedlings. The map shows the number of trees already planted in each of **16** regions of the park.

A student notices that the arrangement of trees planted so far resembles a magic square.

1 Copy and complete the square. How many seedlings need to be planted in each space to make the arrangement a magic square? You can work backward.

2 What will every sum be?

12		14	3
		2	15
1	16	7	10
13	4	11	

CHAPTER PROJECT

The magic star works similar to a magic square. The sum along any line must be **24**.

- Work in groups to find the solution to this magic star.

- Now make your own magic square or magic star. You can use the square or star from this activity to help you get started.

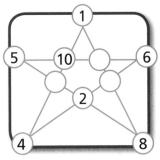

ALMANAC
Fact

Trees help keep the environment clean. An average mature tree will remove about 20 tons of pollution from the air each year.

EXPLORE
Subtracting Magic Squares

The picture shows the addition of magic squares A and B.

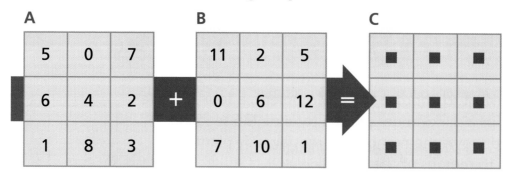

1 Find **C**. Is **C** a magic square?

What happens when B is subtracted from C?

Subtract the number in the upper left box of B from the number in the upper left box of C to find a number in the new grid.

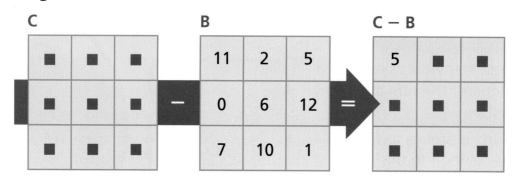

2 Find **C − B**. Is **C − B** a magic square?

---

3 Can you predict what **C − A** will be without doing any additions or subtractions?

---

4 Write a subtraction sentence to show how you get one of the numbers in **C − B**.

---

5 Complete the fact family for the answer to **Problem 4**.

REVIEW MODEL
Subtracting with Magic Squares

The difference of two magic squares is a magic square.

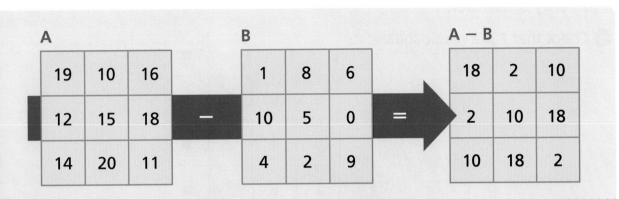

A

19	10	16
12	15	18
14	20	11

B

1	8	6
10	5	0
4	2	9

A − B

18	2	10
2	10	18
10	18	2

Step ❶ Verify the sum of each row, column, and diagonal in A is the same. The sum here is 45. A is a magic square.

Step ❷ Verify the sum of each row, column and diagonal in B is the same. The sum here is 15. B is a magic square.

Step ❸ Find the difference of the numbers in the corresponding boxes of magic squares A and B. Verify the sum of each row, column, and diagonal in A − B is the same. The sum here is 30. A − B is a magic square. Since the sums in A are 45 and the sums in B are 15, the sum of each row, column, and diagonal in A − B is 45 − 15 = 30.

$19 - 1 = 18$	$10 - 8 = 2$	$16 - 6 = 10$
$12 - 10 = 2$	$15 - 5 = 10$	$18 - 0 = 18$
$14 - 4 = 10$	$20 - 2 = 18$	$11 - 9 = 2$

✔Check for Understanding

❶ Find the difference of magic squares D and E and verify the new grid is a magic square.

D

14	5	11
7	10	13
9	15	6

E

6	2	4
2	4	6
4	6	2

D − E

■	■	■
■	■	■
■	■	■

EXPLORE
Multiplying Magic Squares by Numbers

Let's see what happens when you multiply a magic square by a number.

1 Check that **F** is a magic square.

F

5	0	7
6	4	2
1	8	3

Let's multiply **F** by 3. To find the number in the upper left box of the new grid, multiply the number in the same box of **F** by 3. Do the same for each box in the new grid.

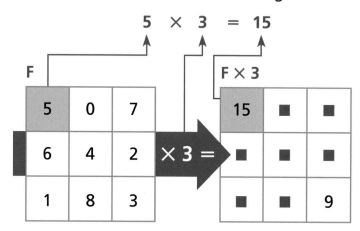

$$5 \times 3 = 15$$

2 Multiply **F** by 3. Is the result a magic square?

3 Do you think the product of a magic square and a number is always a magic square? Why or why not?

REVIEW MODEL
Multiplying a Magic Square by a Number

A product of a magic square and a number is a magic square.

Step ❶

Check that C is a magic square.

The rows, columns, and diagonals all add to 27, so C is a magic square.

C

13	4	10
6	9	12
8	14	5

13	4	10	27
6	9	12	27
8	14	5	27
27	27	27	27

(27)

Step ❷

Multiply C by 4. To find the number in each box in the new grid, multiply the number in the corresponding box by 4. The sum of the rows, columns, and diagonals in C × 4 is 108 which is 4 × 27, the sum in magic square C.

C × 4

52	16	40
24	36	48
32	56	20

✔Check for Understanding _____

❶ Find the product of magic square T and 6.
   Verify it is a magic square.

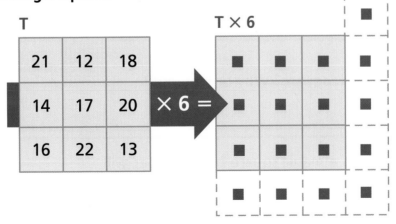

T

21	12	18
14	17	20
16	22	13

× 6 =

T × 6

EXPLORE
Dividing Magic Squares

1 What happens when you divide a magic square by a number?

Complete magic square **K**.

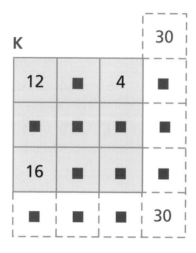

---

2 To find the number in the upper right box of **K ÷ 2**, divide the number in the same box of **K** by **2**.

$$4 \div 2 = 2$$

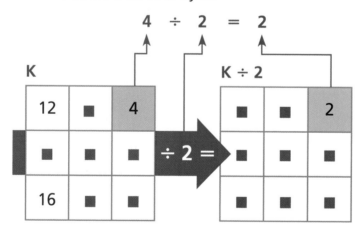

A Find **K ÷ 2.**

B Is the result a magic square? Why or why not?

---

3 Do you think dividing a magic square by a number will always result in a magic square? Why or why not?

EXPLORE
Working Backward to Solve Division Puzzles

Here's a puzzle with magic squares.

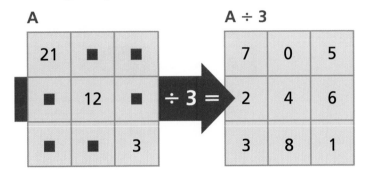

Most of the numbers in the first magic square are missing, but you can use the numbers in the second magic square to help you fill them in.

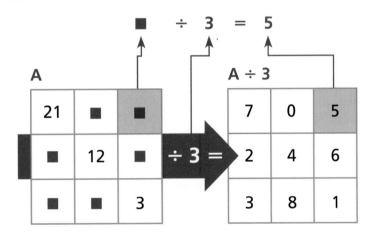

This division sentence shows how to find the number in the upper right box of the magic square.

You can also rewrite it as a multiplication sentence: **3 × 5 = ■**

1 Write a division sentence and a multiplication sentence about the lower left boxes of this puzzle. Does either of these sentences help you figure out what number to fill in the first magic square?

2 Use the numbers in the second magic square to help you complete the first magic square.

REVIEW MODEL
Problem Solving Strategy
Work Backward

Copy the magic squares on paper. Fill in the missing numbers to complete the magic squares.

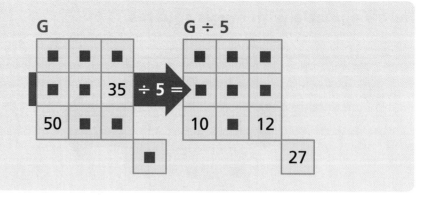

Strategy: Work Backward

Read to Understand

What do you need to find?

I need to fill in the missing numbers so that each is a magic square and the division sentence is correct.

Plan

How can you solve this problem?

I can use the problem solving strategy work backward to fill in some of the missing numbers.

Solve

How can working backward help you find the missing numbers?

I can find the number in the lower right corner by working backward: 12 × 5 = 60. I can also work backward to find the sum of magic square G: 27 × 5 = 135.

Check

Look back at the original problem. Does the answer make sense?

Yes. Each grid is a magic square and the division sentence is correct.

Problem Solving Practice

Use the strategy *work backward* to solve.

1

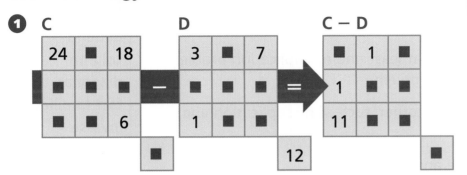

Mixed Strategy Practice

Use any strategy to solve. Explain.

2 Henry has 45 action figure cards. He starts adding 9 more to his collection each week. How many weeks until he has 81 cards?

3 Leonardo is buying 5 pounds of ground meat for $3 a pound and 5 packages of buns for $2 each. If he pays with a $50 bill, how much change should he receive?

For 4–5, use the table.

FAVORITE ICE CREAM FLAVOR	
Flavor	**Number of Students**
Chocolate	■
Mint Chip	54
Strawberry	21
Vanilla	82

Andre surveyed 267 students about their favorite ice cream flavor.

4 How many students picked chocolate as their favorite flavor?

5 Put the ice cream flavors in order from most liked to least liked.

6 The band director had a special stage built for school performances.

What is the area of this stage? Explain what strategy you used and how you solved the problem.

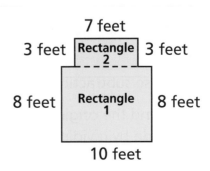

Choose the best vocabulary term from Word List A for each sentence.

1. Multiplication __?__ have at least one multiplication problem and at least one division problem.

2. Operations that undo each other, such as multiplication and division, are __?__.

3. When you multiply, the answer is the __?__.

4. In a magic square, two squares of a __?__ are the lower right square and the upper right square.

5. In a magic square, two squares of a __?__ are the lower right square and the lower left square.

6. A(n) __?__ is one of the numbers being added to make a sum.

7. When you divide, the answer is the __?__.

8. In a magic square, each number in a __?__ is in a different row and column.

Word List A

addend
column
diagonal
fact families
inverse
  operations
lower
product
quotient
right
row
sum

Complete each analogy using the best term from Word List B.

9. Sum is to addition as __?__ is to multiplication.

10. Difference is to sum as __?__ is to product.

Word List B

addend
sum
product
quotient

💬 Talk Math

Describe what you have just learned about magic squares with a partner using the vocabulary terms in Word List A.

11. How can you use subtraction to create a new magic square?

12. How can you find the original magic square if a related magic square was made by dividing each number by 3?

Concept Map

13 Create a concept map for the words describing the positions of the squares of a magic square. Imagine the diagram as 3 rows and 3 columns of a magic square. Use the words *upper, lower, middle, right,* and *left.*

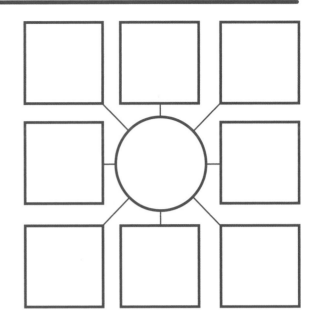

Analysis Chart

14 Create an analysis chart for the terms *addend, sum, product,* and *quotient.*

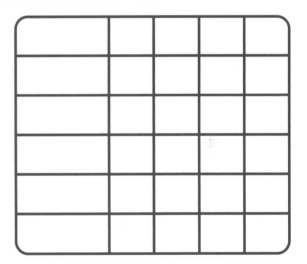

COMMUTATIVE The term *commute* means "to change" or "to exchange one thing for another." Another meaning of *commute* is "to travel back and forth regularly." People generally commute between their homes and work. In mathematics, the term *commutative* means that when you add or multiply, changing the order of the numbers does not change the result.

GAME

Hit the Target!

Game Purpose
To practice addition and subtraction facts

Materials
- Activity Master 5 (*Number Cards*)
- index cards
- stopwatch or clock with second hand

Hit the Target!

How To Play The Game

1 Play this game with a partner. Cut out the number cards from Activity Master 5. Use index cards to make at least two sets of operation cards for +, −, and =.

2 Mix up the number cards and put them face down in a pile. Player 1 turns over the top card. This is the target number.

3 Player 2 turns over 4 more number cards. Player 2 has 1 minute to use all the number cards and any of the +, −, and = cards to make the target number. Player 1 keeps track of the time.

Example: The target number is 8. Player 2 has 2, 1, 6, and 3. Player 2 makes this number sentence and scores 1 point.

$$1 + 3 - 2 + 6 = 8$$

- If Player 2 cannot make a number sentence, Player 1 has 1 minute to try. If successful, Player 1 scores 1 point.
- If neither player can make a number sentence, no point is scored.

4 Put all the cards back together. Mix them up, and switch roles.

5 When time is called, the player with the most points wins.

Number Builder

Game Purpose
To practice facts

Materials
• Activity Master 5 (*Number Cards*)
• index cards
• stopwatch or clock with second hand

How To Play The Game

1 Play this game with a partner. Cut out the number cards from Activity Master 5. Use the index cards to make operation cards for $+$, $-$, $\times$, $\div$, (,), and $=$.

2 Mix up the number cards and put them face down in a pile. Player 1 turns over the top two cards to make a 2-digit number. This is the target number.

3 Turn the rest of the cards face up. Player 2 has 2 minutes to make the target number. The numbers on the cards can be used only as 1-digit numbers. Player 1 keeps track of the time.

Example: The first 2 cards are 1 and 8, so the target number is 18.

(**3** + **7**) × **2** − **6** + **4** = **1** **8**

• If Player 2 cannot make a number sentence, Player 1 has 2 minutes to try. If successful, Player 1 scores 1 point.
• If neither player can make a number sentence, no point is scored.

4 Put all the cards back on the table. Mix them up, and trade roles.

5 When time is called, the player with the most points wins.

CHALLENGE

Frank builds fences. He uses different lengths of logs to build different styles of fences. Below are plans for some of his fences.

Frank has written out one way of finding the total number of logs and the total number of feet he needs for each fence.

Look at the shorter way. Then write the total number of feet.

❶ This fence will have 20 sections like this one.

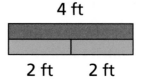

4 ft

2 ft   2 ft

$(20 \times 4) + 20 \times (2 + 2) =$
$20 \times 4 + 20 \times 4 = 20 \times 8 = \blacksquare$ feet

❷ This fence will have 18 sections like this one.

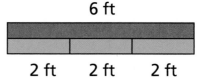

6 ft

2 ft   2 ft   2 ft

$(18 \times 6) + 18 \times (2 + 2 + 2) = \blacksquare$ feet

❸ This fence will have 22 sections like this one.

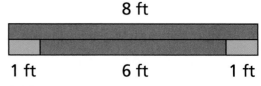

8 ft

1 ft   6 ft   1 ft

$(22 \times 8) + 22 (1 + 1) + (22 \times 6) = \blacksquare$ feet

❹ This fence will have 15 sections like this one.

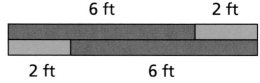

6 ft   2 ft

2 ft   6 ft

$15 \times (6 + 2) + 15 \times (6 + 2) = \blacksquare$ feet

❺ This fence will have 19 sections like this one.

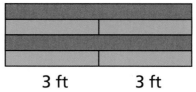

6 ft

3 ft   3 ft

$19 \times (2 \times 6) + 19 \times (4 \times 3) = \blacksquare$ feet

2 Multiplication

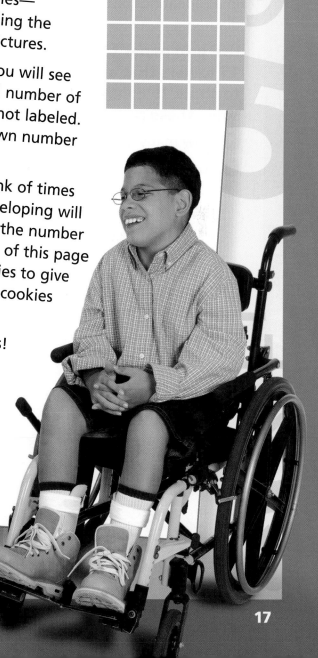

Dear Student,

In this chapter, you will be figuring out the number of dots or tiles in pictures like the ones at the right.

You will develop different strategies—multiplication and more—for finding the number of tiles or dots in these pictures.

Towards the end of the chapter, you will see pictures where you know the total number of tiles, but the rows or columns are not labeled. Your job will be to find the unknown number of columns or rows.

As you go through the chapter, think of times when the strategies you will be developing will be useful. For example, can finding the number of squares in the pictures at the top of this page help you figure out how many cookies to give each of 5 friends when you have 20 cookies to share?

We hope you will enjoy these lessons!

Mathematically yours,
The authors of *Think Math!*

Light Sculptures

FACT·ACTIVITY 1

What a display of lights! If you drive to Los Angeles International Airport (LAX), you are welcomed with an amazing light show of glass towers that change colors every three hours in a repeating pattern. Fifteen 100-foot-tall towers, 12 feet in diameter, and eleven smaller towers make up the display.

Use grid paper to design your own light display. Create 15 towers that are 9 blocks tall. Draw a rectangular array to show 15 columns with 9 blocks each. Use your array to solve these problems.

❶ How many light sections or blocks are there altogether?

❷ Suppose each of your towers is a solid color. You use four colors: purple, blue, red, and orange. Design your array so the number of towers of each color is different.

• How many towers will there be of each color?

• Find the total number of light blocks of each color.

❸ The LAX light display repeats in a three-hour cycle. How many cycles run in one day?

Huge lights show the letters *L-A-X* at the airport. Create a model for the letter *L* to design a new light display. Suppose you want to light 3 rectangular sections using red, white, and blue. Copy the *L* grid shown. Divide the grid into three arrays that will represent the 3 lighting sections.

1 Write a multiplication sentence to represent each array, and determine the number of lights needed to fill each section.

2 What is the total number of lights in the entire display?

3 Suppose your *L* design can have 165 light blocks in all. Draw a 15 × 11 array to represent all the light blocks. Divide it into 4 smaller arrays to verify that the sum of the four products is 165. Hint: Begin with a 10 × 10 array.

CHAPTER PROJECT

Design your own light display of 100 lights on a square grid.

- Use 4 different colors.
- Draw the arrangement so there are 4 rectangular sections.
- Write a multiplication sentence for each smaller array.
- Show how the number of lights in the four arrays add up to 100.

ALMANAC Fact

LAX is one of the world's busiest airports. More than 60 million passengers traveled into or out of LAX in 2005!

EXPLORE
Array Sections

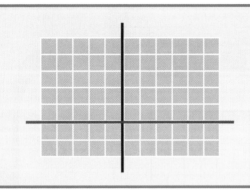

1 Find the number of squares in this array.

2 Explain how you found this number.

3 Copy and complete the diagrams and number sentences to match the array.

A

■	5 × 6
■	■

■	30
■	■

(■ × ■) + (■ × ■) + (5 × 6) + (■ × ■) = ■

B

5 × 11
■

55
■

(■ × ■) + (■ × ■) = ■

C

7 × 5	■

35	■

(■ × ■) + (■ × ■) = ■

REVIEW MODEL
Separating an Array in Different Ways

Find the number of squares in this array.

There are many ways to find the number of squares in an array.

1st Way

Step ❶

Separate the array into four smaller sections, as is done above. The large array is separated into two 4-by-7 arrays and two 3-by-7 arrays.

Step ❷

Complete each table to match the array.

4 × 7	4 × 7
3 × 7	3 × 7

28	28
21	21

Step ❸

Write a number sentence to find the total number of squares in the array.

(4 × 7) + (3 × 7) + (4 × 7) + (3 × 7) = 98

There are 98 squares in this array.

Another Way

Step ❶

Separate the array with only the horizontal line above. The large array is separated into a 4-by-14 array and a 3-by-14 array.

Step ❷

Complete each table to match the array.

4 × 14	56
3 × 14	42

Step ❸

Write a number sentence to find the total number of squares in the array.

(4 × 14) + (3 × 14) = 98

✔Check for Understanding

❶ Find the number of squares in this array. Show your work.

EXPLORE
Combining Multiplication Facts

How many squares are in an array with 6 rows and 18 columns?

1 Copy and complete this table.

	1	2	3	5	6	8	10	11
× 6	■	■	■	■	■	■	■	■

2 Use some of the multiplication facts in the table to separate the array and find the number of squares in each section. Copy and complete the grid and tables in **A** and **B** below.

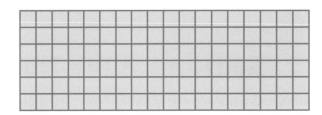

A

6 × 10	■	■

B

60	■	■

3 How many squares are in the array?

4 What is 6 × 18?

REVIEW MODEL
Using an Array to Explore a Multiplication Shortcut

You can use arrays to model a multiplication shortcut.
How many squares are in an array with 4 rows and 17 columns?

Step ❶

Make a table to show multiplication facts you already know about the number of rows or the number of columns in the array.

	1	2	4	5	7	10
× 4	4	8	16	20	28	40

This table is about multiplying by 4 because there are four rows in the array.

Step ❷

Use the facts from the table to decide how to separate your array into smaller sections.

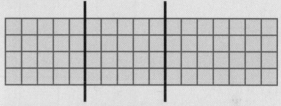

Here the array is separated into three smaller arrays, a 4-by-5 array, a 4-by-5 array, and a 4-by-7 array, since 5 + 5 + 7 = 17.

Step ❸

Using the table from Step 1, find the number of squares in each section of the array.

4 × 5 = 20	4 × 5 = 20	4 × 7 = 28

Step ❹

Find 4 × 17. Add the number of squares from each section of the array to find the total number of squares in the array.

4 × (5 + 5 + 7)
= (4 × 5) + (4 × 5) + (4 × 7)
= 20 + 20 + 28 = 68

There are 68 squares in an array with 4 rows and 17 columns.

✔ Check for Understanding

Find the number of squares in each array. Show your work.

❶ How many squares are in an array with 9 rows and 23 columns?

❷ How many squares are in an array with 7 rows and 19 columns?

EXPLORE
Multiplication Patterns

Copy and complete the multiplication table.

×	1	2	3	4	5	6	7
1							
2							
3							
4							
5							
6							
7							

❶ How could you use the 5-times column to complete the 6-times column?

_____

❷ Choose one of the top two rows and double the answers. What do you notice?

_____

❸ Choose any two of the top four rows and add the answers. What do you notice?

_____

❹ Do you see any other patterns?

EXPLORE
How Many Rows and Columns?

① How many columns are in this array?

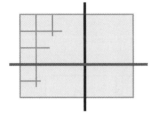

3 × ■	3 × ■
2 × ■	2 × ■

12	9
8	6

---

② How many rows are in this array?

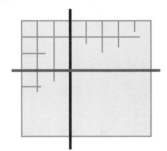

■ × 3	■ × 5
■ × 3	■ × 5

9	15
12	20

---

③ Use 15 tiles to make a rectangular array.

A How many rows does your array have?

B How many columns does your array have?

C Write a multiplication sentence to describe your array.

D Write the fact family that matches your array.

REVIEW MODEL
Finding the Number of Rows or Columns in an Array

You can find the missing dimension of an array by finding the missing factor in multiplication sentences.

How many columns are in this array?

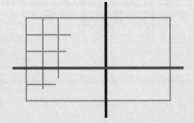

3 × ■	3 × ■
2 × ■	2 × ■

15	12
10	8

Step ❶

Because the array is incomplete, you must find the number of columns by using the tables with the multiplication expressions and the total number of squares in each section of the large array.

Make one table by writing multiplication sentences using the corresponding sections of the array and the tables above.

3 × ■ = 15	3 × ■ = 12
2 × ■ = 10	2 × ■ = 8

Step ❷

Find the missing factor in each multiplication sentence.

3 × 5 = 15	3 × 4 = 12
2 × 5 = 10	2 × 4 = 8

By finding the missing factor in each multiplication sentence, you find the number of columns in each section of the large array.

Step ❸

Since 5 + 4 = 9, there are 9 columns in the large array.

✔ Check for Understanding

❶ How many rows are in this array?

■ × 5	■ × 8
■ × 5	■ × 8

25	40
10	16

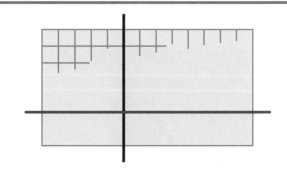

EXPLORE
Arranging 24 Tiles

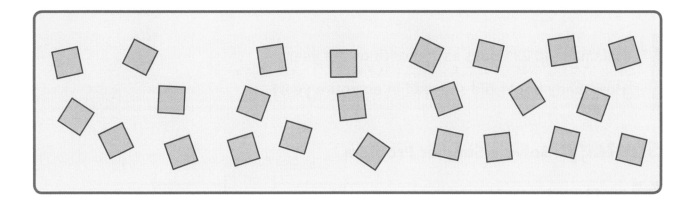

1 Arrange these 24 tiles into an array with 2 columns. How many tiles are in each column?

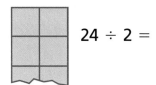 $24 \div 2 =$

2 Now arrange the tiles into an array with 3 columns. How many tiles are in each column?

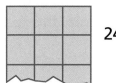 $24 \div 3 =$

3 Now arrange the tiles into an array with 4 columns. How many tiles are in each column?

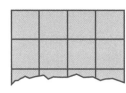 $24 \div 4 =$

4 Now arrange the tiles into an array with 5 columns.

A How many tiles are in each column?

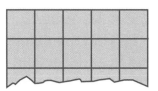

B Can you write a number sentence to describe the array?

REVIEW MODEL
Problem Solving Strategy
Solve a Simpler Problem

Halaina read 23 books each month of the year.

How many books did she read in an entire year?

Strategy: Solve a Simpler Problem

Read to Understand

What do you know from reading the problem?

Halaina read 23 books each month of the year.

Plan

How can you solve this problem?

There are 12 months in one year. You can solve several simpler multiplication problems to find out how many books Halaina read in one year.

Solve

How can you solve simpler problems to solve this problem?

Make a 12-by-23 array. Separate it into smaller sections using multiplication facts you know. For example, you could create 4 sections: 10×12, 2×12, 10×11, and 2×11. Find the number of squares in each section: 120, 24, 110, and 22. Add to find the total number of squares in the large array $120 + 24 + 110 + 22 = 276$. Halaina read 276 books in one year.

Check

Look back at the problem. Did you answer the question that was asked? Does the answer make sense?

Problem Solving Practice

Solve a simpler problem to solve.

Problem Solving Strategies

✔ Act It Out
✔ Draw a Picture
✔ Guess and Check
✔ Look for a Pattern
✔ Make a Graph
✔ Make a Model
✔ Make an Organized List
✔ Make a Table
✔ **Solve a Simpler Problem**
✔ Use Logical Reasoning
✔ Work Backward
✔ Write an Equation

1 Staci uses 36 beads in each necklace that she makes. She made 11 necklaces. How many beads did she use?

2 Rob washes 6 cars each week. How many cars does he wash in 23 weeks?

Mixed Strategy Practice

Use any strategy to solve.

3 Mrs. Holmes' class made kites. She hung her students' kites in the hallways. She had 2 rows of 7 kites in one hall and 2 rows of 4 kites in another hall. How many kites were displayed in all?

4 Todd has baseball practice from 3:30 P.M. to 4:30 P.M. It takes him a half hour to get home. Then he has one hour to eat his dinner before he must start his homework. At what time does he start his homework?

5 Adele, Denise, Ron, and Tom are all standing in line in the cafeteria. How many different ways can they arrange themselves to stand in line?

6 Aidan won the same number of tickets at each of the 3 games he played at the fair. His sister gave him 5 more tickets. If Aidan then has 23 tickets, how many tickets did he win at each game he played?

Use pattern blocks for Problems 7–8.

7 Alycia made a trapezoid using 3 red trapezoids, 1 blue rhombus, and 1 green triangle. What other combination of pattern blocks can be used to make a trapezoid congruent to the one Alycia made?

8 Use a different combination of pattern blocks to make another congruent trapezoid.

Choose the best vocabulary term from Word List A for each sentence.

Word List A

array
column
divide
division
factor
factor pairs
horizontal line
leftover
missing factor
remainder
remaining
row
variable
vertical line

1 A(n) __?__ problem can be rewritten as a division sentence.

2 An operation related to multiplication is __?__.

3 Multiply __?__ to find a product.

4 In a division problem, the r stands for __?__.

5 A letter that can stand for a number is called a(n) __?__.

6 A number that is multiplied by another number to find a product is a __?__.

7 A column is part of a(n) __?__.

8 When there are __?__ tiles, it means that there is a remainder.

Complete each analogy using the best term from Word List B.

Word List B

array
column
factor
variable

9 Addend is to sum as __?__ is to product.

10 Horizontal line is to vertical line as row is to __?__.

Talk Math

Discuss with a partner what you have learned about multiplication and division. Use the vocabulary terms *array*, *column*, and *row*.

11 How can you use an array to model multiplication?

12 How can you use an array to model division?

13 A large array of dots is separated into two smaller arrays. How can you find the total number of dots?

Venn Diagram

14 Create a Venn diagram for multiplication terms and division terms. Use the words *array, column, divide, division, factor, factor pairs, leftover, missing factor, product, remainder, remaining,* and *row.*

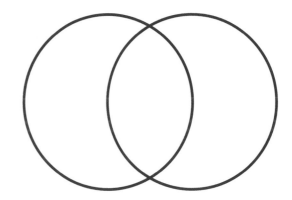

Word Definition Map

15 Create a word definition map using the word *division.* Use what you know and what you have learned about multiplication and division.

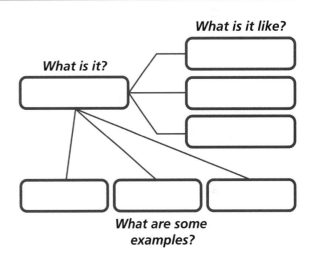

What is it like?

What is it?

What are some examples?

PRODUCT The word *product* can be used in many different situations. The *product* of a farm might be corn, beans, wheat, milk, or beef. Those things are produced on a farm. The *product* of a factory might be cars, marbles, baseball bats, or light bulbs. Those things are produced in a factory. Similarly, in mathematics a product is produced by multiplying two or more numbers.

GAME

Array Builder

Game Purpose
To practice using arrays as a model for multiplying

Materials
• Activity Master 8: *Array Builder*
• 2 different colors of crayons or pencils
• a coin

How to Play the Game

1 Play this game with a partner. Before starting, make a 1 × 2 array on the *Array Builder* by shading the two upper left squares. Choose your crayon color. Then decide who will play first.

2 Player 1 flips the coin.
• If the coin lands heads up, add 1 row or column to the array.
• If the coin lands tails up, add 2 rows or columns to the array.
• Try to make an array that will give the largest product. Your score for that turn is the product for the array.

Example: The first 4 possible plays of the game are shown in red.

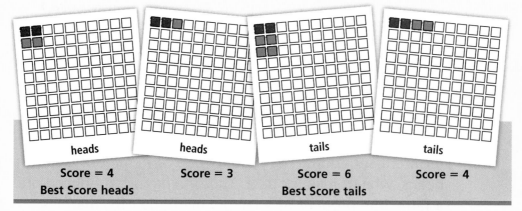

heads	heads	tails	tails
Score = 4	Score = 3	Score = 6	Score = 4
Best Score heads		Best Score tails	

3 Take turns flipping the coin and making new arrays until there are not enough squares left to make a play.

4 Add your points. The player with the most points is the winner.

GAME

Fact Family Fandango

Game Purpose
To practice writing multiplication and division fact families

Materials
• 2 number cubes (labeled 1–6)

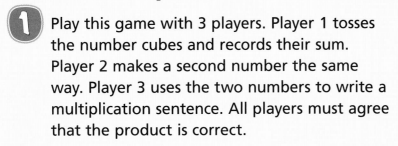

How to Play the Game

1 Play this game with 3 players. Player 1 tosses the number cubes and records their sum. Player 2 makes a second number the same way. Player 3 uses the two numbers to write a multiplication sentence. All players must agree that the product is correct.

Example:

John tosses these numbers.

Charlie tosses these numbers.

Nancy writes this multiplication sentence.

$8 \times 10 = 80$

2 Next, each player secretly writes another member of the fact family for that multiplication sentence.

3 Compare all 3 multiplication sentences. You score **1** point if you wrote a number sentence that no one else wrote.

Example: Here are the multiplication and division sentences that John, Charlie, and Nancy wrote.

So, Charlie scores **1** point.

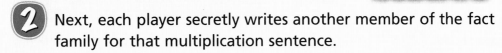

John
$8 \times 10 = 80$

Charlie
$80 \div 8 = 10$

Nancy
$8 \times 10 = 80$

4 Switch roles, and repeat steps 1 through 3. Play until one player scores **10** points and wins the game.

CHALLENGE

Cheryl likes to share. Help solve each of her problems so that she can share evenly with no leftovers.

You may want to use counters, tiles, or coins to make arrays.

Cheryl wants to share her raisins. When she tries to share them with one friend, there is 1 left over. When she tries to share them with 2 friends, there are 2 left. When she tries to share them with 3 friends, there is 1 left. When she tries to share them with 4 friends, there are 4 left. (Remember that Cheryl herself shares with each group.)

1 Does Cheryl have an odd number or an even number of raisins? How do you know?

2 What is the smallest number of raisins Cheryl could be trying to share?

3 What is the smallest number of raisins she should have next time so that she can share them evenly with 1, 2, 3, or 4 friends?

Cheryl has a box of crayons. The table below shows what happens when she tries to share them.

When she tries to share them with	there are (is)
1 friend	none left over
2 friends	1 left over
3 friends	2 left over

4 Does Cheryl have an odd number or an even number of crayons? How do you know?

5 What is the smallest number of crayons she could be trying to share?

6 What is the smallest number of extra crayons she should have next time so that she can share them evenly with 1, 2, or 3 friends?

Chapter

3 The Eraser Store

Dear Student,

In this chapter, you will be working at an Eraser Store where special containers are used for packaging the erasers.

There are two rules used in the store. One rule is that packs, boxes, and crates must be full. The other rule is that there must be as few containers and as few loose erasers as possible in each shipment.

You will be developing important mathematical skills as you answer questions such as:

How many erasers are in 1 box?

How many erasers are in 1 crate?

What packages will be used to fill an order for 25 erasers?

As you go through these lessons, try to think about strategies for doing these computations in your head. You may be surprised that you can add 49 + 49 + 49 + 49 without any paper!

We hope you enjoy your time in the store, and that you keep track of all your orders!

Mathematically yours,
The authors of *Think Math!*

7 erasers to a pack

7 packs to a box

7 boxes to a crate

How Many Can You Eat?

Does the county you live in have a fair? If so, the fair may have an eating contest for adults. One popular contest is hot dog eating.

FACT·ACTIVITY 1

Use the data from the table below to answer the questions.

Results From Hot Dog Eating Contest	
Contestant	**Number of Hot Dogs Eaten in 12 Minutes**
A	51
B	48
C	36
D	34
E	34

❶ How many hot dogs were eaten by the top two contestants altogether?

❷ How many more hot dogs did the winner eat than Contestant C?

❸ If Contestant E had eaten twice as many hot dogs, would Contestant E have won the contest? Explain.

❹ Suppose a contestant ate 27 hot dogs in 9 minutes. On the average, how many hot dogs would the contestant have eaten per minute?

Organizers of hot dog eating contests need to purchase many hot dogs for the contestants and for the spectators. They can have hot dogs shipped to them in packages, boxes, or crates. There are 8 hot dogs in a package, 8 packages in a box, and 8 boxes in a crate.

1 Did Contestant A eat more than a box of hot dogs? Explain.

2 How many packages of hot dogs and single hot dogs did Contestant C eat?

3 How many hot dogs are in a crate?

4 If 1,000 hot dogs were eaten, write the number of crates, boxes, packages, and single hot dogs used.

CHAPTER PROJECT

Plan a party for a number of guests you would like to invite. Determine the number of packages of hot dogs, buns, and bottles of water needed for the party. Make a table to show the information.

Background information for the project:

You want enough food so every person at the party will have at least 2 hot dogs, 2 buns, and 1 bottle of water.

The food is packaged in this way:
- 8 hot dogs per package, 8 packages in a box
- 6 hot dog buns per package, 6 packages in a box
- 6 bottles of water per pack, 4 packs in a case

Determine the total number of
- boxes and packages of hot dogs. (Assume that you cannot buy individual hot dogs.)
- boxes and packages of buns. (Assume that you cannot buy individual buns.)
- packs, cases, and individual bottles of water. (Individual bottles of water can be purchased.)

ALMANAC
Fact

According to the International Federation of Competitive Eating, the record for most hot dogs eaten in 12 minutes is $53\frac{3}{4}$, achieved in 2006 in Coney Island in Brooklyn, New York.

REVIEW MODEL
Introducing the Eraser Store

You can find the number of crates, boxes, and packs that are needed to package a shipment of erasers at the Eraser Store.

How many of each type are needed for a shipment of 465 erasers?

Remember: • **7 erasers to a pack**   • **7 packs to a box**   • **7 boxes to a crate**

Step ❶ Find the number of crates needed.

1 crate will hold $7 \times 7 \times 7 = $ **343** erasers.

2 crates will hold $2 \times 343 = $ **686** erasers

465 is between 343 and 686, so **1 crate** is needed.

$$\begin{array}{r} 465 \\ -\ 343 \\ \hline 122 \end{array}$$ erasers left over

Step ❷ Find the number of boxes needed.

1 box will hold $7 \times 7 = 49$ erasers.

2 boxes will hold $2 \times 49 = $ **98** erasers.

3 boxes will hold $3 \times 49 = $ **147** erasers.

122 is between 98 and 147, so **2 boxes** are needed.

$$\begin{array}{r} 122 \\ -\ 98 \\ \hline 24 \end{array}$$ erasers left over

Step ❸ Find the number of packs needed.

1 pack will hold 7 erasers.

3 packs will hold $3 \times 7 = $ **21** erasers.

4 packs will hold $4 \times 7 = $ **28** erasers.

$$\begin{array}{r} 24 \\ -\ 21 \\ \hline 3 \end{array}$$ **erasers** left over.

24 is between 21 and 28, so **3 packs** are needed.

So, 465 erasers can be packaged in 1 crate, 2 boxes, 3 packs, and 3 loose erasers.

✔Check for Understanding

Find the number of each type of package for each shipment of erasers.

❶ 597 erasers

❷ 357 erasers

❸ 97 erasers

❹ 228 erasers

EXPLORE
Order Form

The Eraser Store sells:

- loose erasers   — packs of 7 erasers
- ▢ crates of 7 boxes   ▢ boxes of 7 packs

Here's an order form received at the store:

Total Number of Erasers	▢ ▢ — •
360	1 , 0 , 2 , 3

1 What does the **3** below the dot mean?

_____

2 What does the **2** below the line mean?

_____

3 What does the **0** below the square mean?

_____

4 What does the **1** below the cube mean?

_____

5 Why do you think the numbers are separated by commas?

EXPLORE
Changing Shipment Orders

Elizabeth ordered 2 packs and 6 loose erasers.

1 Use linkable cubes to represent this order. Make **2 rods** of **7 cubes** and **6 loose cubes.**

2 Elizabeth **increased** her order by **1 pack** and **5 erasers.** Use linkable cubes to represent this additional order.

3 How should the whole order be packaged?

Daniel ordered 4 packs and 2 loose erasers.

4 Use linkable cubes to represent this order.

5 Daniel **decreased** his order by **2 packs** and **5 loose erasers.** Use linkable cubes to represent the resulting shipment when these erasers are removed.

6 Describe the shipment Daniel received.

REVIEW MODEL
Combining and Reducing Shipments

You can find the new number of packages needed for a shipment after an order increased at the Eraser Store.

Remember: • **7 erasers to a pack** • **7 packs to a box** • **7 boxes to a crate**

Step 1 Add and repackage loose erasers.

   5 loose erasers in the top order
+ 5 loose erasers in the bottom order
─────
  10 total loose erasers

= 1 pack of 7 erasers + **3** loose erasers

	1	1	3	5
+	0	3	3	5
				3

Step 2 Add and repackage the packs.

   3 packs in the top order
   3 packs in the bottom order
+ 1 new pack formed
─────
  7 total packs

= 1 box with **0** packs

	1	1	3	5
+	0	3	3	5
			0	3

Step 3 Add and repackage the boxes and crates.

   1 box
   3 boxes   1 crate
+ 1 new box   + 0 crates
─────   ─────
  5 boxes   1 crate

	1	1	3	5
+	0	3	3	5
	1	5	0	3

✔Check for Understanding

Find the number of each type of package for each shipment of erasers.

1

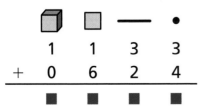

	1	1	3	3
+	0	6	2	4
	■	■	■	■

2

	1	1	3	3
+	0	3	4	6
	■	■	■	■

EXPLORE
Packaging Multiple Identical Shipments

**The Eraser Store is still shipping:
10 erasers in a pack, 10 packs in a box, and 10 boxes in a crate.**

A school ordered 1 pack and 3 erasers for each of 4 classes.

1 Use base-ten blocks to represent the order for one class.

2 Use base-ten blocks to represent the school's total order.

3 How many erasers were in the total order?

A store ordered 3 packs and 5 erasers for each of its 6 locations.

4 Use base-ten blocks to represent one order.

5 Use base-ten blocks to represent the store's total order.

6 How many erasers were in the total order?

REVIEW MODEL
Multiple Shipments

You can find the new number of packages needed for a shipment when multiple identical orders are made at the Eraser Store. Remember: 10 erasers in a pack, 10 packs in a box, and 10 boxes in a crate.

Multiply: 5 × 0 crates, 1 box, 2 packs, 7 loose erasers

Step ❶ Multiply and repackage the loose erasers.

| 7 loose erasers × 5 orders | = 35 loose erasers |
| | = **3** packs + **5** loose erasers |

Write **5** as the new number of loose erasers.

$$\begin{array}{r} \overset{\overset{3}{}}{0,\,1,\,2,7} \\ \times \quad\quad 5 \\ \hline 5 \end{array}$$

Step ❷ Multiply and repackage the packs.

2 packs × 5 orders	= 10 packs
Add 3 packs from Step 1: 10 + 3	= 13 packs
	= **1** box + **3** packs

Write **3** as the new number of packs.

$$\begin{array}{r} \overset{1\ \ \overset{3}{}}{0,\,1,\,2,7} \\ \times \quad\quad 5 \\ \hline 3,5 \end{array}$$

Step ❸ Multiply and repackage the boxes.

1 box × 5 orders	= 5 boxes
Add 1 box from Step 2: 5 + 1	= 6 boxes
	= **0** crates + **6** boxes

Write **6** as the new number of boxes. Zero crates are needed.

The total number of packages is 0, 6, 3, 5.

$$\begin{array}{r} \overset{1\ \ \overset{3}{}}{0,\,1,\,2,7} \\ \times \quad\quad 5 \\ \hline 0,6,3,5 \end{array}$$

✔ Check for Understanding

Multiply.

❶
$$\begin{array}{r} 1,\,0,\,2,\,1 \\ \times \quad\quad 7 \\ \hline \end{array}$$

❷
$$\begin{array}{r} 0,\,2,\,6,\,8 \\ \times \quad\quad 5 \\ \hline \end{array}$$

❸
$$\begin{array}{r} 2,\,4,\,5,\,7 \\ \times \quad\quad 3 \\ \hline \end{array}$$

EXPLORE
Separating Packages of Erasers

The Eraser Store is still packaging:

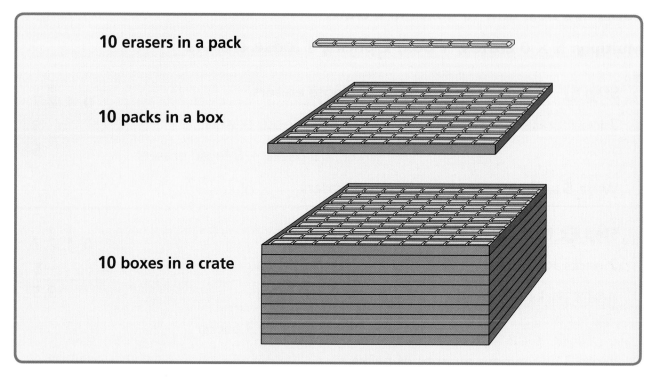

10 erasers in a pack

10 packs in a box

10 boxes in a crate

Dana, Joel, and Rachel ordered a total of 3 boxes, 4 packs, and 2 loose erasers. They decided to share the erasers in the shipment equally.

1 Use base-ten blocks to represent the total order.

_____

2 Use base-ten blocks to represent what Dana gets.

_____

3 How many erasers does Dana get?

_____

4 How did you divide the total order among 3 people?

REVIEW MODEL
Dividing Shipments

You can find the new number of packages needed for a shipment when orders are divided equally at the Eraser Store.

Divide: $4 \overline{| \, 0, 6, 5, 2}$

Step 1 Divide the crates into equal groups.

Zero crates divided into 4 groups gives 0 crates in each group.

$$\begin{array}{r} 0 \\ 4 \overline{| \, 0, \ 6, \ 5, \ 2} \end{array}$$

Step 2 Divide and repackage the boxes, if necessary.

6 boxes divided into 4 groups gives **1** box in each group, with 2 boxes left over. Open the 2 boxes to make 20 packs. Add them to the 5 packs that are already there: $20 + 5 = \mathbf{25}$. Write a **2** beside the 5.

$$\begin{array}{r} 0, \ 1 \\ 4 \overline{| \, 0, \ 6, \ ^25, \ 2} \end{array}$$

Step 3 Divide and repackage the packs, if necessary.

25 packs divided into 4 groups gives **6** packs in each group, with 1 pack left over. Open the pack to make 10 loose erasers. Add them to the 2 loose erasers already there: $10 + 2 = \mathbf{12}$. Write a **1** beside the 2.

$$\begin{array}{r} 0, \ 1, \ 6, \\ 4 \overline{| \, 0, \ 6, \ ^25, \ ^12} \end{array}$$

Step 4 Divide the loose erasers.

12 loose erasers divided into 4 groups gives **3** erasers in each group.

$$\begin{array}{r} 0, \ 1, \ 6, \ 3 \\ 4 \overline{| \, 0, \ 6, \ ^25, \ ^12} \end{array}$$

The total number of erasers in each order after division is 163.

✔ Check for Understanding

Divide.

1 $3 \overline{| \, 1, 4, 6, 4}$

2 $2 \overline{| \, 2, 4, 7, 4}$

3 $6 \overline{| \, 1, 5, 4, 8}$

EXPLORE
Shipments Without Commas

> **The Eraser Store is still packaging:**
> **10 erasers in a pack, 10 packs in a box, and 10 boxes in a crate.**

Mr. Zeh ordered erasers for his school, but some commas are gone from the order!

Order Form	Mr. Zeh: **4,183**

1 How many erasers are in a crate?

2 How many erasers are in a box?

3 How many erasers are in a pack?

4 Copy and complete this number sentence to find the total number of erasers in Mr. Zeh's order.

$4 \times \blacksquare + 1 \times \blacksquare + 8 \times \blacksquare + 3 = \blacksquare$

5 What do you notice about the order form and the number of erasers in Mr. Zeh's order?

Mrs. Ray also ordered erasers for her school.

Order Form	Mrs. Ray: **6,935**

6 How many erasers did she order?

7 Copy and complete this number sentence:

$6 \times \blacksquare + 9 \times \blacksquare + 3 \times \blacksquare + 5 = \blacksquare$

8 How many total erasers did Mr. Zeh and Mrs. Ray order?

EXPLORE
Rounding Shipments

José ordered 784 erasers and his sister, Rosa, ordered 694 erasers.

1 Did José order closer to **700** or **800** erasers?

2 Did Rosa order closer to **600** or **700** erasers?

3 Together, about how many erasers did José and Rosa order?

Kiko ordered 2,115 erasers, but her mom reduced the order by 322 erasers.

4 Round Kiko's original order to the nearest **hundred**.

5 Round **322** to the nearest **hundred**.

6 Estimate the number of erasers that Kiko will receive.

Each of Stacy's 9 friends ordered 53 erasers.

7 Round **53** to the nearest **ten**.

8 Use your rounded number to estimate **53 × 9**.

Derrick reduced his eraser order of 2,394 by 1,476 erasers.

9 Estimate Derrick's final order.

10 If Derrick and his 4 friends share his erasers, about how many erasers will each get?

REVIEW MODEL
Problem Solving Strategy
Make a Table

Gershon was preparing an order for the Eraser Store. He didn't write down how many crates or boxes were in the order or how many total erasers were ordered. His notes said that the order would include a total of **11 containers**, **4 of which were packs**, and there would be **no loose erasers**. How many different combinations of containers could there be in Gershon's order?

Strategy: Make a Table

Read to Understand

What do you know from reading the problem?

The order included **11** containers. Four of those containers were packs. There were no loose erasers.

Plan

How can you solve this problem?

Think about the strategies you might use. One way is to make a table.

Solve

How can you make a table?

Make a row or column for each type of container. List all the combinations that satisfy the requirements of the problem.

_____ total of 11 containers

_____ 4 packs

_____ no loose erasers

There are **8** combinations that answer the question.

Check

Look back at the problem. Did you answer the questions that were asked? Does the answer make sense?

Crate	Box	Pack —	Eraser •
7	0	4	0
0	7	4	0
6	1	4	0
1	6	4	0
5	2	4	0
2	5	4	0
4	3	4	0
3	4	4	0

Problem Solving Practice

Use the strategy _make a table_ to solve.

Problem Solving Strategies

✔ Act It Out
✔ Draw a Picture
✔ Guess and Check
✔ Look for a Pattern
✔ Make a Graph
✔ Make a Model
✔ Make an Organized List
✔ **Make a Table**
✔ Solve a Simpler Problem
✔ Use Logical Reasoning
✔ Work Backward
✔ Write an Equation

1 Tracy had 16¢ in her pocket. How many different combinations of coins could she have?

2 Joey tosses two number cubes, each numbered 1–6. How many different ways can the numbers have a sum of 7?

Mixed Strategy Practice

Use any strategy to solve. Explain.

3 Kate had two bags of prizes to give to each of her party guests. There were 6 more prizes in the first bag than in the second bag, and a total of 38 prizes in both bags. Find the number of prizes in each bag.

4 Jason jumped 6.2 meters on his first jump at a track meet. On his second jump, he jumped 0.45 meters farther. What was the total combined length of his two jumps?

5 The 19 members of the swim team each swam 8 laps. How many total laps did the team swim?

6 Trina spent $4\frac{1}{4}$ hours studying for her tests, $2\frac{1}{4}$ hours running errands, and $1\frac{1}{2}$ hours working out in the lawn. She also spent some time exercising. If she spent 11 hours in all, how long did she exercise?

7 How many scores are possible if you toss 2 beanbags onto the game board shown?

1	3
7	5

8 Ryan's average score on 2 tests was 89. He scored 95 on the first test. What did he score on the second test?

Choose the best vocabulary term from Word List A for each sentence.

Word List A

bar graph
chart
comma
divided by
estimate
inverse
multiple
multiplication
multiply
packing
repacking
round
symbol
unpacking

1 A table or a graph is a type of __?__ that displays data.

2 The number 12 is a __?__ of 3.

3 To add 4 + 4 + 4 + 4 + 4, you can __?__ 4 by 5.

4 Addition and subtraction are __?__ operations.

5 The __?__ that represents the operation "add" is +.

6 A(n) __?__ is an approximation.

7 A(n) __?__ uses vertical or horizontal bars to display data.

8 To __?__ is to find a number near a given number that is easier to compute with.

Complete each analogy using the best term from Word List B.

Word List B

chart
estimate
multiplication
symbol

9 Subtraction is to addition as division is to __?__.

10 Daisy is to flower as bar graph is to __?__.

Talk Math

Discuss with a partner what you have learned about regrouping. Use the vocabulary terms *packing*, *repacking*, and *unpacking*.

11 An Eraser Store packs erasers by the base-7 system. How can you combine two orders of erasers?

12 An Eraser Store packs erasers by the base-10 number system. It has 1,000 erasers. How can you find the number of erasers left after an order is filled?

Concept Grid

14 Create a degrees of meaning grid that includes the terms *bar graph*, *chart*, *estimate*, and *round*.

General	Less General	Specific

Word Web

15 Create a word web using the word *multiplication.* Use what you know and what you have learned about multiplying and multiplication.

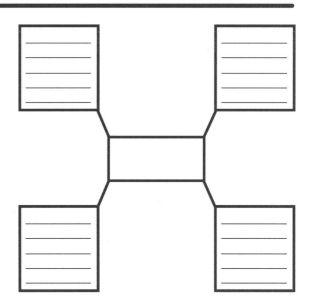

SYMBOL, CYMBAL The words *symbol* and *cymbal* sound the same even though they have different spellings. They also mean different things. A cymbal is a musical instrument. Cymbals are large plates made of bronze or brass. They can make a loud clashing sound when struck, or they can make a soft ting if tapped lightly.

A *symbol* is a sign used to stand for something else. Much of mathematics is written in *symbols* that are understood in many countries of the world. For example, almost everyone understands what 5 + 3 means. *Symbols* help make mathematics a universal language.

GAME

Eraser Inventory

Game Purpose
To practice combining and reducing shipments in the base-ten system

Materials
• Number cube (1–6)
• Activity Master 15: Eraser Inventory

Eraser Inventory

How To Play The Game

1 This is a game for 2 players. Each player will need one number cube and a copy of AM15: Eraser Inventory. The Eraser Store has 5 crates of erasers in stock. They accept only orders smaller than a crate.

2 Player 1 tosses the number cube three times.
• Toss 1 is the number of boxes in the order.
• Toss 2 is the number of packs in the order.
• Toss 3 is the number of loose erasers in the order.

3 Player 1 records the shipment in the spaces for Shipment #1.

4 Player 2 then figures out how many crates, boxes, packs, and loose erasers remain in stock. Player 2 records the numbers in the spaces for "New amount in stock."

5 Switch roles. Player 2 repeats Steps 2 and 3, and Player 1 repeats Step 4.

Example: Player 1 rolls 4, 6, 1. Then Player 2 rolls 2, 5, 6.

In stock	5 , 0 , 0 , 0
Shipment #1	4 , 6 , 1
New amount In stock	4 , 5 , 3 , 9
Shipment #2	2 , 5 , 6
New amount In stock	4 , 2 , 8 , 3

6 Keep taking turns until one player rolls an order that is too large to fill. The last player able to have his or her order filled wins!

GAME

Least to Greatest

Game Purpose
To practice estimation

Materials
- Activity Masters 17–18: Least to Greatest Cards
- Stopwatch or clock with a second hand

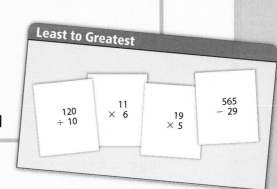

Least to Greatest

120 ÷ 10

11 × 6

19 × 5

565 − 29

How To Play The Game

1 Play this game with a partner. Cut out the *Least to Greatest* cards from Activity Masters 17 and 18.

2 Choose one player to be the Placer and the other to be the Timer.
- The Placer holds all the *Least to Greatest* cards face down in a stack.
- The Timer gets ready to time the Placer for **60** seconds.

3 The goal is to place as many cards as possible in order from least to greatest. The Timer tells the Placer when to start. The Placer turns over one card at a time and places it where it belongs in a line of cards. Since you have only **60** seconds, a good strategy is to estimate rather than to calculate exactly.

4 When the 60 seconds are up, the Timer checks the cards.
- The Timer solves the problem on each card to see whether the cards are in the correct order.
- If the Timer finds an error, the Placer can remove cards from the row so the remaining cards are in order.
- When the order of the cards is correct, the Placer gets 1 point for each card in the line.

5 Switch roles, and play again. Keep a running tally of your points. The first player to reach **50** wins!

CHALLENGE

The Eraser Store wants to experiment with other ways of packing erasers. They will still sell loose erasers, but they will now put 8 in a pack, 8 × 8, or 64 in a box, and 8 × 8 × 8, or 512 in a crate.

For example, to send 925 erasers, they will use

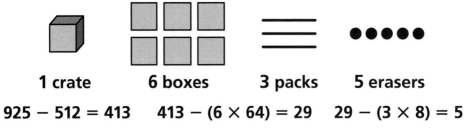

| 1 crate | 6 boxes | 3 packs | 5 erasers |

$$925 - 512 = 413 \qquad 413 - (6 \times 64) = 29 \qquad 29 - (3 \times 8) = 5$$

The Eraser Store has 5 orders to fill. The shipping clerk has filled the number of crates for each order. Copy and complete each order.

	Order	🧊	🟦	—	●
1	155 erasers				
2	400 erasers				
3	605 erasers	🧊			
4	1,000 erasers	🧊			
5	715 erasers	🧊			

Chapter

4 Classifying Angles and Figures

Dear Student,

In this chapter, you will be learning new names for some figures that may already be familiar to you and names for some figures that may not be.

See how many of these you can name. Can you think of 2 different names for figure C? Can you think of a way to tell figures A, E, and G apart? Can you find something similar among figures C, F, and H?

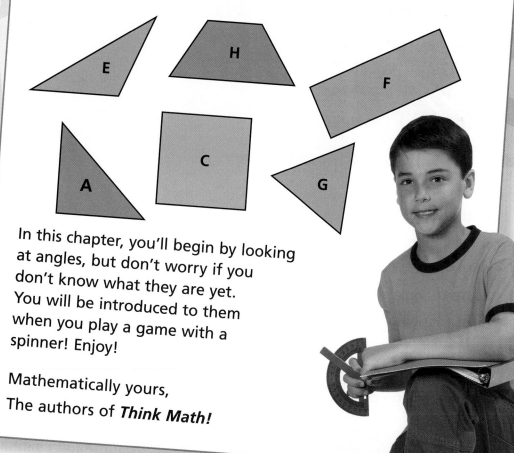

In this chapter, you'll begin by looking at angles, but don't worry if you don't know what they are yet. You will be introduced to them when you play a game with a spinner! Enjoy!

Mathematically yours,
The authors of **Think Math!**

Bridge Geometry

FACT·ACTIVITY 1

Triangular shapes are very important in construction because they can support a lot of weight. That's why you might see a lot of triangles when you look at a bridge. What other shapes and angles do you see in bridges?

1. Use the bridge photos above. Write the number that identifies the geometric term.

   • parallel lines

   • perpendicular lines

   • acute triangle

   • right triangle

   • obtuse triangle

2. Describe and draw three more geometric figures you see in the bridge photos.

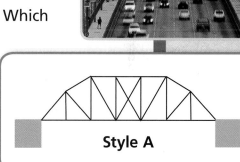

The Golden Gate Bridge, like many bridges, is symmetric. The Golden Gate Bridge is a suspension bridge, the roadway hangs from a series of interconnected cables.

The suspension bridge is just one of many different styles of bridges. Two others are shown below. Although they look different, they each contain similar geometric shapes and properties.

1. Copy or trace bridge Style A. Outline and name two types of triangles and two types of quadrilaterals in the bridge.

2. Which style, A or B, has only one line of symmetry? Which has two lines of symmetry? Explain.

3. The top half of Style B looks like it may be resting on a mirror. What term can be used to describe the two parts of the bridge?

4. Make a drawing of a bridge that includes the following features:

   • parallel lines
   • perpendicular lines
   • congruent triangles
   • symmetry

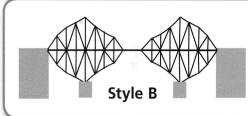

Style A

Style B

CHAPTER PROJECT

Materials: straws or craft sticks (no more than 30), tape, glue, scissors

Work in groups of four. Your group must:

• Agree on a design of a bridge. Use the drawings from Fact Activity 2 to help. Design the bridge to demonstrate symmetry, parallel and perpendicular lines, and other geometry concepts taught in this chapter.

• Next, build the bridge to match your design.

• Write a description of your bridge explaining its geometric features.

ALMANAC Fact

As of June 2005, almost 2 billion vehicles had crossed the Golden Gate Bridge. There are more than 600,000 rivets in each bridge tower.

EXPLORE
Angles in Triangles

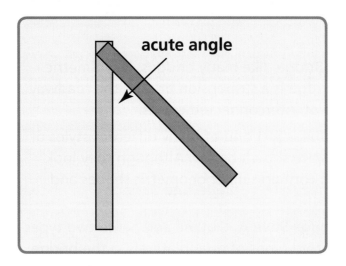

acute angle

Sketch the triangles you make on a piece of scratch paper.

1 Use 3 strips of paper to try to make a triangle with **3 acute angles.**

Is this possible?

_____

2 Now use the strips of paper to try to make a triangle with exactly **2 acute angles.**

Is this possible?

_____

3 Now try to make a triangle with only **1 acute angle.**

Is this possible?

REVIEW MODEL
Using Equal Sides to Make Triangles

You can make a triangle with 0 equal sides. The triangle can be an acute triangle, a right triangle, and an obtuse triangle.

Acute and Scalene	**Right and Scalene**	**Obtuse and Scalene**
3 sides are not same length; 3 acute angles	3 sides are not same length; 1 right and 2 acute angles	3 sides are not same length; 1 obtuse and 2 acute angles

You can make a triangle with exactly 2 equal sides. The triangle can be an acute triangle, a right triangle, and an obtuse triangle.

Acute and Isosceles	**Right and Isosceles**	**Obtuse and Isosceles**
2 sides are equal 3 acute angles	2 sides are equal 1 right and 2 acute angles	2 sides are equal 1 obtuse and 2 acute angles

You can make a triangle with exactly 3 equal sides. The triangle can be an acute triangle. You cannot make a triangle with exactly 3 equal sides and form a right triangle or an obtuse triangle.

Acute and Equilateral
3 sides are equal
3 acute angles

✔ Check for Understanding

1 What are the different classes for triangles using angles and side lengths?

2 Can you make an obtuse equilateral triangle? What kinds of triangles are impossible?

EXPLORE
Sorting Parallelograms

Write the letter(s) of the figures that belong in the third group on a separate piece of paper.

1 All of these belong.   None of these belong.   Which of these belong?

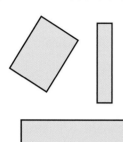
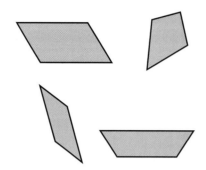
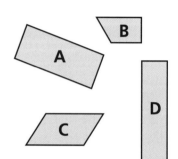

---

2 All of these belong.   None of these belong.   Which of these belong?

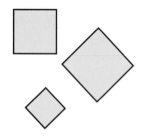
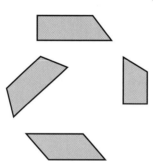
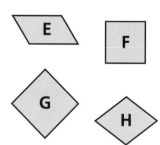

---

3 All of these belong.   None of these belong.   Which of these belong?

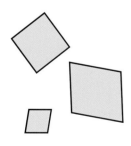
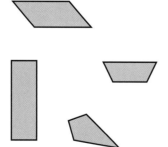
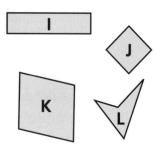

---

4 Draw a figure that belongs to all 3 groups on a separate sheet of paper.

REVIEW MODEL
Classifying Parallelograms

Parallelograms are quadrilaterals with 2 pairs of parallel sides. Some parallelograms are rectangles and some are rhombuses.

A rectangle is a parallelogram with 4 right angles. These are rectangles:

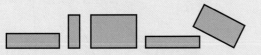

A rhombus is a parallelogram with 4 sides of equal length. These are rhombuses:

A square can also be called a rectangle because it has 4 right angles. It is a special rectangle because it also has 4 sides of equal length. All squares are rectangles, but not all rectangles are squares.

A square is also a rhombus because it has 4 sides of equal length. It is a special rhombus because it also has 4 right angles.

All squares are rhombuses, but not all rhombuses are squares.

✔Check for Understanding

On a separate sheet of paper write T if the statement is TRUE. Write F if the statement is FALSE.

1 All squares are parallelograms.

2 All parallelograms are squares.

3 Some parallelograms are either rectangles or rhombuses.

4 Some rhombuses are squares.

5 All squares are rhombuses.

EXPLORE
Symmetry in Classes of Triangles

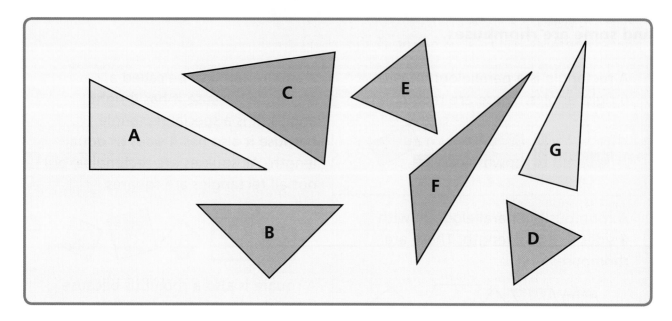

1 Which **have no lines of symmetry?**

What kind of triangles are these?

___

2 Which triangles have exactly **1 line of symmetry?**

What kind of triangles are these?

___

3 Which triangles have **3 lines of symmetry?**

What kind of triangles are these?

___

4 Can you find any triangles with **exactly 2 lines of symmetry?**

REVIEW MODEL
Transformations of a Triangle

These three types of transformations do not change the size and shape of the original figure.

Translation

A translation, or slide, moves a figure without changing its orientation. The direction of movement is shown by an arrow.

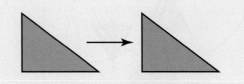

Reflection

A reflection, or flip, flips a figure over a line so that the new and the original figures are mirror images of each other over the line. The line is shown as dotted.

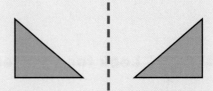

Rotation

A rotation, or turn, moves a figure around a fixed point that is chosen. It is shown by a point on the figure.

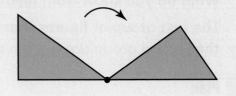

✔Check for Understanding

❶ Translate, reflect, and rotate this triangle. Draw these transformations on a separate sheet of paper.

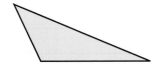

REVIEW MODEL
Problem Solving Strategy
Look for a Pattern

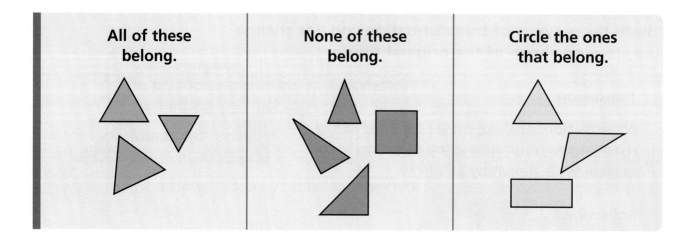

| All of these belong. | None of these belong. | Circle the ones that belong. |

Strategy: Look for a Pattern

 Read to Understand

What do you know from reading the problem?

The first group of figures share characteristics the second group doesn't have.

Plan

How can you solve this problem?

by figuring out which figure in the third group shares characteristics with those in the first group

 Solve

How can you look for a pattern?

The figures that belong are all equilateral triangles. The figures that do not belong are isosceles triangles, scalene triangles and quadrilaterals. So, the equilateral triangles are the figures that belong.

 Check

Look back at the problem. Did you answer the question that was asked? Does the answer make sense?

Problem Solving Practice

Use the strategy _look for a pattern_ to solve.

❶ What could be the missing figure in the pattern? Explain.

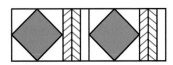

❷ Tina made this design. What part of the pattern comes next? Explain.

Problem Solving Strategies

✔ Act It Out
✔ Draw a Picture
✔ Guess and Check
✔ **Look for a Pattern**
✔ Make a Graph
✔ Make a Model
✔ Make an Organized List
✔ Make a Table
✔ Solve a Simpler Problem
✔ Use Logical Reasoning
✔ Work Backward
✔ Write an Equation

Mixed Strategy Practice

Use any strategy to solve. Explain.

❸ At a carnival, Alonso and his friends paid $1 for 3 pictures at a photo booth. They had a total of 18 pictures taken. How much money did they spend on pictures?

❹ Eli buys 3 books that each cost $1.97. The clerk adds $0.35 in sales tax. Eli pays using bills and receives less than a dollar as change. How much did Eli pay the clerk?

Use the table.

❺ How many large yards does Rafael need to mow to earn the same amount of money he earns mowing 6 medium yards?

LAWN MOWING EARNINGS	
Yard Size	**Amount Earned**
Small Yard	$23
Medium Yard	$35
Large Yard	$42

❻ These figures are all quadrilaterals.

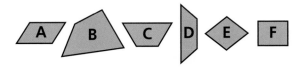

Sort the figures into a Venn diagram drawn on a separate sheet of paper.

QUADRILATERALS

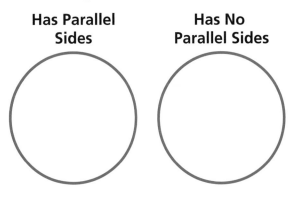

Has Parallel Sides   Has No Parallel Sides

Choose the best vocabulary term from Word List A for each sentence.

1 A triangle with no equal sides is called a(n) __?__.

2 Two intersecting lines that form right angles are __?__.

3 A figure that has exactly four sides is a(n) __?__.

4 Lines that do not cross and are the same distance apart from each other are called __?__.

5 An angle that is smaller than a right angle is a(n) __?__.

6 A __?__ has 4 sides that are the same length.

7 Any quadrilateral that has two pairs of parallel sides is called a(n) __?__.

8 A mathematical term for flipping a figure is __?__.

9 A triangle that has two or more equal sides is called a(n) __?__.

10 Turning a figure is the same as __?__ it.

Complete each analogy using the best term from Word List B.

11 Flipping is to reflecting as sliding is to __?__.

12 Equilateral triangle is to triangle as __?__ is to quadrilateral.

Talk Math

Discuss with a partner what you have just learned about classifying figures. Use the vocabulary terms *line of symmetry*, *obtuse angle*, *right angle*, *acute angle*, and *parallel lines*.

13 How can you describe an equilateral triangle?

14 How can you describe a square?

15 How can you describe a trapezoid?

Word List A

acute angle
acute triangle
equilateral
  triangle
interseacting
  lines
isosceles
  triangle
obtuse angle
parallel lines
parallelogram
perpendicular
  lines
quadrilateral
reflecting
rhombus
rotating
scalene triangle
sliding
trapezoid

Word List B

angle
square
translating
turning

Degrees of Meaning Grid

16 Create a degrees of meaning grid for the terms *quadrilateral* and *triangle.*

General	Less General	Specific

Tree Diagram

17 Create a tree diagram using the word *transformation.* Use what you know and what you have learned about translating, rotating, and reflecting figures.

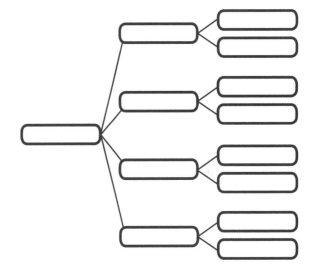

What's in a Word?

SQUARE Words often have more than one meaning. Some words, such as *square,* even have more than one mathematical meaning. A *square* is a quadrilateral with four right angles and four equal sides. Area is measured in square units, such as "4 *square* inches." Here is another use of the word *square.* To *square* a number means to multiply the number by itself; for example, 4×4 is 4 squared (4^2) or 16.

Figure Bingo

Game Purpose
To practice identifying attributes of figures and lines

Materials
- Activity Master 27 (*Figure Bingo*)
- Activity Master 28 (*Bingo Figures*)
- Activity Master 29 (*Bingo Cards*)

How To Play The Game

1 Play this game with a small group. Each group will need one set of *Bingo Cards*. Each player will need a *Figure Bingo* page and one set of *Bingo Figures*.

2 Pick one student to be the Caller. The Caller cuts out the *Bingo Cards* for the group.

3 Players cut out their *Bingo Figures* along the dotted lines. Place them face-up in any order on your *Figure Bingo* page.

4 The Caller picks a *Figure Card* from the pile and reads it aloud. Look at your *Figure Bingo* page. Find any figures that match the description and turn them face-down.

5 Continue playing. The first player to get 5 *Bingo Figures* face-down in a row, column, or diagonal, says "Bingo!"
- If the figures match the descriptions that have been read, that player wins!
- If the figures do not match the descriptions, keep playing until someone else says "Bingo!" and has the correct figures.

6 Choose a new Caller, and play another game.

GAME

Who Has . . . ?

Game Purpose
To practice classifying figures and angles

Materials
• Activity Masters 34 and 35
  (*Who Has . . . Game* cards)

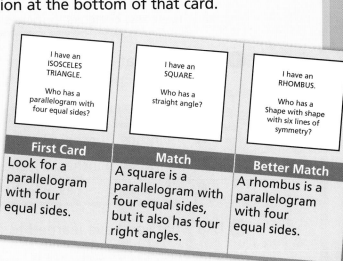
Who Has . . . ?

How To Play The Game

1 Play this game with a small group. Cut out the cards from Activity Masters 34 and 35. Mix them up. Give an equal number of cards to each player.

• If there is an extra card, the person who gets that card is Player 1.

• If there is no extra card, the player who has the card that says "I have a PENTAGON" is Player 1.

2 Player 1 puts down the card face-up and reads the description at the bottom of the card.

3 The player who has the card that best matches the description puts it down, and reads the description at the bottom of that card.

Example:

4 Continue playing in this way. The player whose card best matches the definition puts down the card and reads the next definition aloud.

5 The winner is the first player to match all of his or her cards.

I have an ISOSCELES TRIANGLE. Who has a parallelogram with four equal sides?	I have an SQUARE. Who has a straight angle?	I have an RHOMBUS. Who has a Shape with shape with six lines of symmetry?
First Card	**Match**	**Better Match**
Look for a parallelogram with four equal sides.	A square is a parallelogram with four equal sides, but it also has four right angles.	A rhombus is a parallelogram with four equal sides.

CHALLENGE

Is there a pattern in the lengths of triangle sides? To find out, you will need notebook paper or straws, a pair of scissors, and an inch ruler.

1 Cut 2 strips of paper, or straws, for each of these lengths: 2 inches, 3 inches, 4 inches, 5 inches, 6 inches, 8 inches, 9 inches.

2 Copy the table below. Then try to make each triangle with your paper strips or straws. Record your results in the table. Write *yes* or *no* to tell whether you could make a triangle. Only write *yes* if 3 paper strips or straws make a triangle without overlapping or leaving any gaps.

These are NOT triangles:

	Lengths of Strips	Can I make a triangle?
A	2 inches, 2 inches, 3 inches	
B	2 inches, 3 inches, 5 inches	
C	4 inches, 5 inches, 8 inches	
D	5 inches, 6 inches, 9 inches	
E	3 inches, 4 inches, 8 inches	
F	2 inches, 4 inches, 6 inches	
G	6 inches, 8 inches, 9 inches	

3 Now use what you know to predict whether you will be able to make these triangles. Then test your predictions.

	Lengths of Strips	Can I make a triangle?
H	4 inches, 8 inches, 9 inches	
J	5 inches, 5 inches, 8 inches	
K	3 inches, 3 inches, 9 inches	

4 Use what you have learned to answer this question:

• In order for three sides to form a triangle, what must be true about the sum of the lengths of any two sides?

5 Area and Perimeter

Dear Student,

You already know various units for measuring different kinds of things. If you want to know how long a fence is, you might measure its length in feet and inches.

What units could you use to measure how much water it takes to fill up your bathtub?

What units could you use to measure how much paint is needed to cover a wall?

Would you use the same units to measure the distance around a baseball field?

In this chapter, you'll be measuring with square units of various sizes, like this one:

What could you measure with this unit?

Mathematically yours,
The authors of *Think Math!*

Reading and Analyzing Maps

FACT·ACTIVITY 1

Pictures from satellite cameras above the earth can show your neighborhood. Images can show things as small as 2 meters, such as a bicycle in a park. A map also represents a view from above. The map at the right shows a neighborhood park.

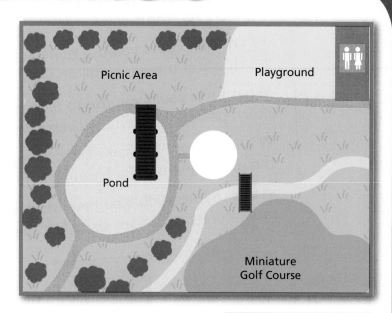

Use the map and a centimeter ruler to answer Problems 1–5.

❶ Find the dock and the bridge on the map. About how many times longer is the dock than the bridge?

❷ To the nearest centimeter, how long is the dock on the map?

❸ If each centimeter represents 10 meters, about how long is the actual dock?

❹ Measure the perimeter of the gazebo with string. To the nearest centimeter, how many centimeters of string did you use?

❺ If each centimeter on the map represents 10 meters, about how many meters is the distance around the gazebo?

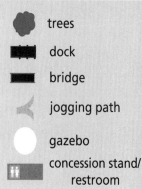

trees

dock

bridge

jogging path

gazebo

concession stand/ restroom

Maps have "legends" that show what measure on the map represents what distance. This map shows that 1 centimeter represents 10 meters. This map also has a grid that helps you estimate measurements.

Look at the park again. Now it is covered by a grid.

1 About how many square meters is the gazebo? Explain.

2 Estimate the area of the pond.

3 Compare the area of the playground to the area of the miniature golf course.

4 Estimate the perimeter of the playground and rest room building. Explain how you found your answer.

5 If each square represents 100 square meters, about how many square meters does the playground cover?

1 cm = 10 meters

Picnic Area   Playground

Pond

Miniature Golf Course

CHAPTER PROJECT

You and your classmates are organizing a club to raise awareness of the need to keep the local park clean. One of your jobs is to create a design that will represent your club.

• Design an emblem for a patch that can be sewn or ironed onto a shirt. The emblem must be no bigger than 28 square centimeters.

• Draw your emblem on centimeter grid paper. Estimate the area of your design.

• Put the club name or motto on the design.

ALMANAC
Fact

The first satellite photos of earth were taken in 1960. They were used to look at weather patterns.

EXPLORE
Comparing Areas

For each pair of figures, decide whether the two figures are congruent, and find the area of each figure. On a separate sheet of paper write *true* or *false* and the area of each figure.

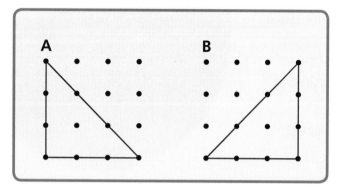

A is congruent to **B**.

True or False

Area of **A**: square units

Area of **B**: square units

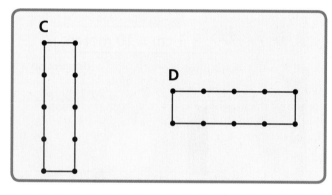

C is congruent to **D**.

True or False

Area of **C**: square units

Area of **D**: square units

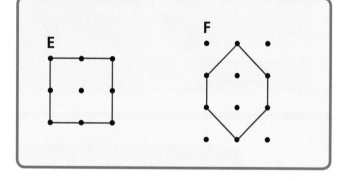

E is congruent to **F**.

True or False

Area of **E**: square units

Area of **F**: square units

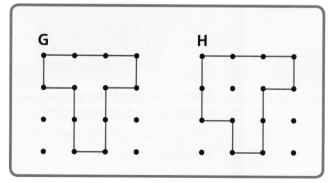

G is congruent to **H**.

True or False

Area of **G**: square units

Area of **H**: square units

REVIEW MODEL
Using Transformations to Find Areas

If two figures are congruent, they must have the same area. The figures will always be congruent if one figure is a reflection, a translation, or a rotation of the other.

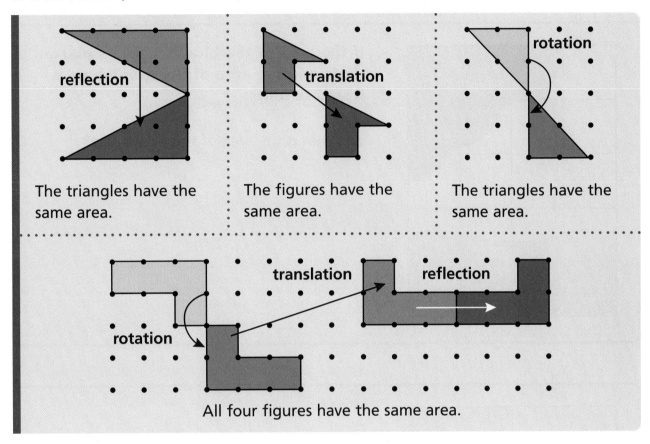

The triangles have the same area.

The figures have the same area.

The triangles have the same area.

All four figures have the same area.

✔ Check for Understanding

Determine if a translation, rotation, or reflection was used to move one figure onto the other. Write your answers on a separate sheet of paper.

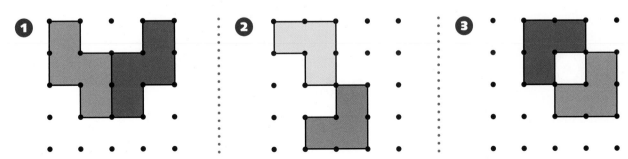

❶   ❷   ❸

EXPLORE
Finding the Area of a Strange Shape

On this page, one unit of area is this big:

Write your answers on a separate sheet of paper.

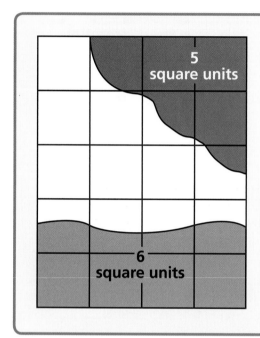

If the area of the blue part is 5 square units and the area of the green part is 6 square units:

1 What is the area of the **white part**?

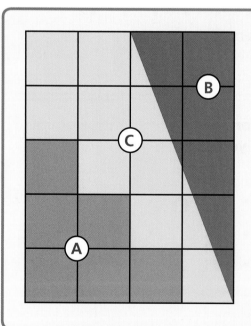

2 What is the area of **A**?

3 What is the area of **B**?

4 What is the area of **C**?

REVIEW MODEL
Finding Areas of Triangles

You can use what you know about finding the area of a rectangle to find the area of a triangle.

What is the area of the shaded triangle?

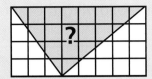

Step ❶

Find the area of the rectangle.

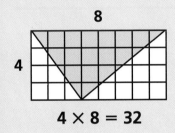

$4 \times 8 = 32$

Step ❷

Find the area of the unshaded triangle on the left.

$(4 \times 3) \div 2 = 6$

Step ❸

Find the area of the unshaded triangle on the right.

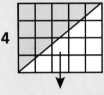

$(4 \times 5) \div 2 = 10$

Step ❹

Subtract the areas of the unshaded triangles from the area of the rectangle.

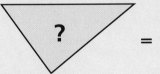   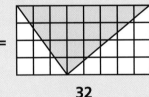

$32 \quad - \quad 6 \quad - \quad 10 \quad = 16$

The area of the shaded triangle is 16 square units.

✔Check for Understanding

Find the area of the shaded triangle. Write your answers on a separate sheet of paper.

❶
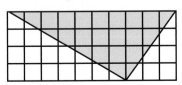

❷
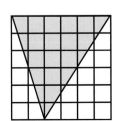

EXPLORE
Making Rectangles Whose Perimeter is 20 cm

1 On a piece of centimeter grid paper, draw as many different rectangles as you can, following these rules:

> **The perimeter is 20 cm.**
>
> **The length of each side must be a whole number of centimeters.**
>
> ✓ **Congruent rectangles all count as the same rectangle.**

2 Find the area of each of your rectangles. (One square of grid paper equals one square centimeter.) Write your answers on a separate sheet of paper.

3 Do you think you've made all the rectangles that can be made following these rules? How could you check?

REVIEW MODEL
Comparing Areas and Perimeters

Area measures the region *inside* a figure. Perimeter measures the distance around the *outside* of the figure.

Two figures can have the **same** perimeter but **different** areas.

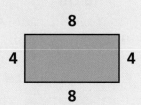

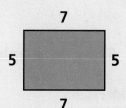

Perimeter = 8 + 4 + 8 + 4 = 24 units

Perimeter = 7 + 5 + 7 + 5 = 24 units

Area = 8 × 4 = 32 square units

Area = 7 × 5 = 35 square units

Two figures can have the **same** area but **different** perimeters.

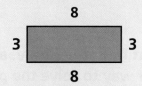

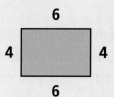

Area = 8 × 3 = 24 square units

Area = 6 × 4 = 24 square units

Perimeter = 8 + 3 + 8 + 3 = 22 units

Perimeter = 6 + 4 + 6 + 4 = 20 units

✔Check for Understanding

Tell if the areas are the same or different. Then tell if the perimeters are the same or different. Write your answers on a separate sheet of paper.

1

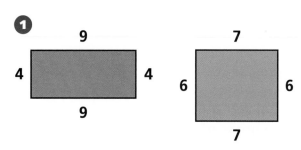

2

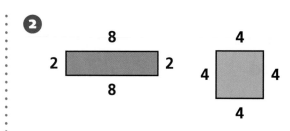

REVIEW MODEL
Problem Solving Strategy
Solve a Simpler Problem

Tony is making large block letters for a class project. His letter U is shown at the right. What is the area of the paper he will need to make the letter?

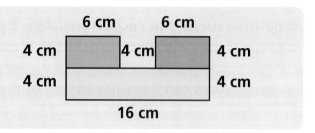

Strategy: Solve a Simpler Problem

 Read to Understand

What do you know from reading the problem?
the dimensions of a figure in the shape of the letter U
What do you need to find out?
the area of the paper needed to make the letter

 Plan

How can you solve this problem?
You could find the areas of the three rectangles that form the figure, and then find their sum. But you could also look for a simpler way to solve the problem.

 Solve

How can a simpler problem help you find the answer?
The green and blue rectangles are the same height as the yellow rectangle. So you could

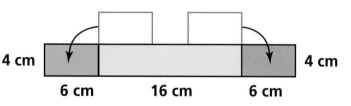

place them beside the yellow rectangle to form a long rectangle 4 cm tall and (6 + 16 + 6) centimeters = 28 centimeters long.

The area of the new rectangle is the same as the area of the letter U. The area is 4 × 28 = 112 square centimeters.

 Check

Look back at the original problem. Does your answer make sense?
If I want to check my answer, I can calculate the areas of the three rectangles individually, and add them to see if I get a sum of 112 square centimeters

Problem Solving Practice

Use the strategy *solve a simpler problem* to solve.

Problem Solving Strategies

✔ Act It Out
✔ Draw a Picture
✔ Guess and Check
✔ Look for a Pattern
✔ Make a Graph
✔ Make a Model
✔ Make an Organized List
✔ Make a Table
✔ **Solve a Simpler Problem**
✔ Use Logical Reasoning
✔ Work Backward
✔ Write an Equation

1 If you draw 2 horizontal and 2 vertical lines, you can make a 9-space tic-tac-toe diagram. If you used 7 horizontal and 7 vertical lines, how many spaces would the diagram have?

2 A bell rang 12 times. Each ring lasted 5 seconds. There were 2 seconds between rings. How long did the ringing last?

Mixed Strategy Practice

Use any strategy to solve. Explain.

3 Greg, Juan, and Valerie found a box of tennis balls. Greg took half the balls. Juan took half of the balls that were left. Valerie took the remaining 3 balls. How many tennis balls were in the box at the beginning?

4 Tiffany and Ted live on the same street. Each of their house numbers has two digits. The sum of the digits of each number is 14. Both numbers are even. What are the house numbers?

5 A snail is at the bottom of a well that is 30 feet deep. Each day the snail crawls up 3 feet. Each night it slips back 2 feet. How long will it take the snail to crawl out of the well?

6 Three darts hit the dartboard. How many scores are possible?

7 Marcus earned $80 in two days. The second day he earned $10 more than he earned the first day. How much did he earn each day?

8 A square has a perimeter of 32 centimeters. What is the area of the square?

Choose the best vocabulary term from Word List A for each sentence.

Word List A

area
centimeter
congruent
estimate
length
meter
perimeter
square units
width

❶ Two figures that have the same size and shape are ___?___.

❷ The distance around a shape is its ___?___.

❸ The top of a card table could have an area of 1 square ___?___.

❹ Area is measured in ___?___.

❺ You can use a stamp to ___?___ the area of a post card in square centimeters.

❻ The number of congruent squares that fit inside a shape is its ___?___.

❼ A(n) ___?___ is not as long as an inch.

❽ To find the area of a rectangle, multiply its length by its ___?___.

Complete each analogy. Use the best term from Word List B.

Word List B

area
centimeter
length

❾ Inch is to perimeter as square inch is to ___?___.

❿ Penny is to dollar as ___?___ is to meter.

Talk Math

Discuss with a partner what you have just learned about area and perimeter. Use the vocabulary terms *length,* *width,* **and** *area.*

⓫ Explain how you could estimate the area of a desktop.

⓬ Explain how you could find the area of the rectangle without including the area of the small triangle.

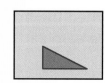

Word Definition Map

14 **Create a Word Definition Map for the word *estimate*.**

A What is it?

B What is it like?

C What are some examples?

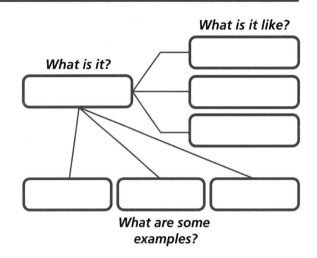

What is it?

What is it like?

What are some examples?

Analysis Chart

15 **Create an analysis chart for the words *centimeter*, *meter*, *inch*, and *foot*. Use what you know and what you have learned about units of measure.**

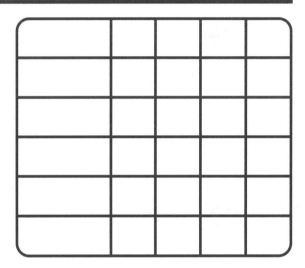

What's in a Word?

METER The original meaning of the word *meter* is "measure." A parking *meter* measures the time a car is parked. A *meter* in poetry is the rhythm of the syllables. A *meter* in music is the number of beats in each musical measure. In each of these examples, *meter* has something to do with "measure."

In mathematics, the *meter* is the basic unit of measure in the metric measurement system. Since the prefix *centi-* means "hundredth," a centimeter is one hundredth of a meter. The prefix *peri-* means "around," so a *perimeter* is the measure around a shape.

GAME

Area 2

Game Purpose
To practice drawing figures with a given area

Materials
• Activity Master 38: *Grid Paper*
• Geoboards (if available)

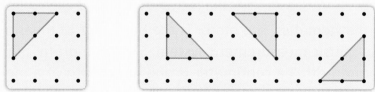

How To Play The Game

1 Play this game with a group. Each player will need several copies of Activity Master 38. Players can also use a geoboard and rubber bands to practice making figures.

2 The first player tries to draw a figure with an area of 2 square units. The group checks to see whether the area is 2 square units. If it is, the player scores 1 point.

3 Players take turns drawing figures with an area of 2 square units. To score 1 point, a player must draw a different figure from the ones that have already been drawn.

Here are some possible figures:

hexagon   pentagon   parallelogram   trapezoid

4 A figure that is a flip, slide, or turn of another figure is not a different figure. So, the player does not get a point.

Example:

Dorian draws this figure. Then these figures cannot score points:

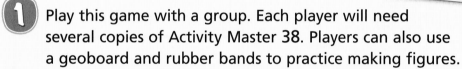

5 The player with the most points is the winner.

GAME

Area Claim

Game Purpose
To practice transforming figures

Materials
- AM39: *Area Claim*, AM40: *Area Claim: Figure Cards*,
  AM41: *Area Claim: Transformation Cards*

How To Play The Game

1 This game can be played with 2 or more players. You need 4 copies of Activity Master 40. Cut out the Figure and Transformation Cards. Mix up the Figure and Transformation Cards. Place them face down in separate piles.

2 Player 1 takes one card from each pile and matches his or her figure card to the same figure on the *Area Claim* grid.

- Look at the Transformation Card. Draw a copy of the figure. Don't overlap any other figure.
- Claim the area by writing your initials in the new figure.
- Put the used cards aside in separate piles.

3 Players take turns adding new figures to the grid.

- You may only start from a figure printed on the grid or from a figure with your initials.
- If the cards run out, mix up the used cards, and keep playing until you go through both piles of cards twice.
- If you cannot find space to draw a new figure, your turn ends.

4 The game ends when there is no room to draw any new figures. Score 1 point for every square unit covered by a figure with your initials. The player with the most points wins.

CHALLENGE

On a geoboard, the shortest line you can make is **1** unit, so the smallest square has an area of **1** square unit.

The largest square you can make will fill the geoboard and have an area of **16** square units.

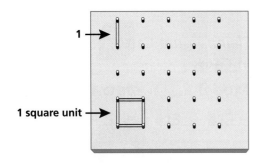

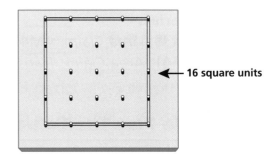

How many squares with different areas between 1 square unit and 16 square units can you make?

Use a geoboard. Or you can trace copies of the board below and draw all the squares with different areas you can make.

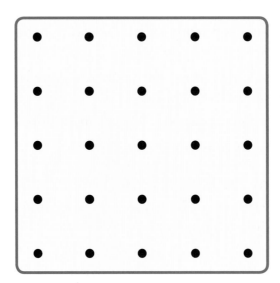

Hint: You will not be able to find squares for every number between 1 and 16.

Chapter

6 Multi-Digit Multiplication

Dear Student,

This chapter is about multiplying big numbers. Can you think of situations when you've used multiplication in class or outside of school?

As you work through the multiplication problems in this chapter, you will be seeing pictures like these, which may remind you of the ones you saw in the previous chapter.

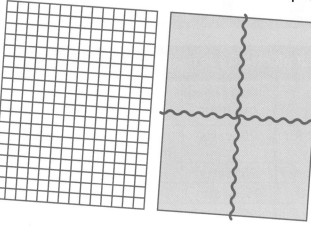

How might these pictures be related to multiplication?

Of course you already know a lot about multiplication. You will have a chance to use what you know to complete multiplication puzzles. Enjoy!

Mathematically yours,
The authors of *Think Math!*

Watt's Up?

We depend on electricity for many things, for example to power appliances. Electricity is usually generated by burning fossil fuels, such as coal and oil. When fossil fuels are used up, they cannot be replaced. We can conserve those fossil fuels by using less electricity. The standard unit of measurement for electrical power is the watt. The table shows the amount of power needed to operate some electric devices for one hour.

FACT·ACTIVITY 1

How much electricity is used?

Energy used per hour	Device	Energy used per hour	Device
5000 watts	Electric oven (800 for a range burner)	20 watts	Desktop computer & monitor (in sleep mode)
3500 watts	Central air conditioner	75 watts	Regular light bulb
1500 watts	Toaster (four-slot)	165 watts	Video game box
1000 watts	Window unit air conditioner	90 watts	19" television
700 watts	Refrigerator	18 watts	Compact fluorescent light bulb
240 watts	Desktop computer & monitor (running)	4 watts	Clock radio

1 Estimate the energy used by a 19" television in 12 hours.

2 Dorian plays a video game box for 3 hours. Estimate the energy used.

3 Which uses more energy in one hour, 12 regular light bulbs or 50 compact fluorescent light bulbs?

4 Justine claims that a computer in running mode uses 12 times more energy than a computer in sleep mode. Is she correct? Explain.

One power plant can produce enough electricity for **540,000** people. That amount of energy would be enough for **180,000** homes with an average of **3** people per home. For which of these Texas cities could one power plant produce enough electricity?

Population of Some Texas Cities	
City	Population
Arlington	362,805
Austin	690,252
Corpus Christi	283,474
El Paso	598,590
Fort Worth	624,047
Temple	55,447

FACT·ACTIVITY 2

Use the population data to answer.

❶ Round each population so that it can be written as a multiple of **100**.

❷ Write the rounded population of Temple as the product of **100** and a whole number.

❸ Write the rounded population of Corpus Christi as the product of **100** and a whole number.

❹ The population of Austin is about **690,000**. Write the rounded population of Austin as the product of **100** and two whole numbers. ■ × ■ × 100 = ■

CHAPTER PROJECT

How much energy could we save? Choose a total of 5 electric devices that you or your family use regularly. Create a table which would show how many watts of power could be saved in a year if the device is used for 1 less hour a day, every day. You may use a calculator to help with the calculations.

For example: Using the television for 1 less hour a day would save 90 watts of electricity every day. This means that you could save 90 × 365 (days in a year) = 32,850 watts per year. Add this savings to the others to find total savings. Present your results in a pamphlet that will promote energy savings. Write a slogan for your pamphlet.

EXPLORE
Multiples of 10 and 100

1 Which of the numbers below can be made by **multiplying** a whole number by **10**?

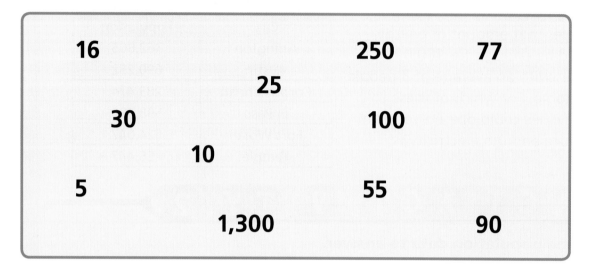

16   250   77

25

30   100

10

5   55

1,300   90

Use **base-ten blocks** to show that these numbers are **multiples of 10**.

---

2 Which of the numbers below can be made by **multiplying** a whole number by **100**?

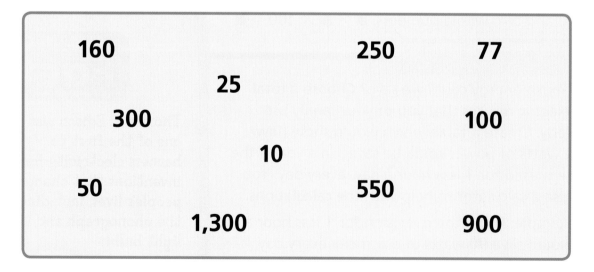

160   250   77

25

300   100

10

50   550

1,300   900

Use **base-ten blocks** to show that these numbers are **multiples of 100**.

REVIEW MODEL
Using Arrays to Model Multiplication

You can use an array and a chart to model multiplication. You can break a number into the sum of two smaller numbers to use simpler multiplication and find a product.

Step ❶ Fill in the boxes with the number of rows and columns that make up the two parts of the array.

$18 \times 4 = \blacksquare$

This is an 18 × 4 array that is divided into an 8 × 4 array and a 10 × 4 array.

4

8

10

Step ❷ Fill in the chart by adding the numbers above the thick line.

This chart shows that you are splitting 18 into 8 + 10.

×	4
8	
10	
18	

Step ❸ Fill in each cell above the thick line by multiplying the numbers in its rows and columns.

This shows that you can solve simpler problems to find products of larger numbers.

×	4
8	32
10	40
18	

Step ❹ Fill in the remaining cells of the chart by adding the two numbers above it.

$(8 \times 4) + (10 \times 4) = 72$, so $18 \times 4 = 72$

×	4
8	32
10	40
18	72

✔ Check for Understanding

Copy the chart and fill in the missing parts.

❶ $17 \times 5 =$

×	5
8	■
9	■
■	■

❷ $19 \times 3 =$

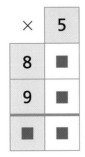

×	3
11	■
8	■
■	■

REVIEW MODEL
Splitting Larger Arrays

You can break an array into four parts and use simpler problems to solve a multi-digit multiplication problem.

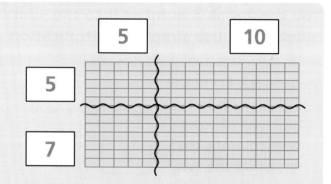

Step 1 Fill in the boxes with the number of rows and columns that make up the four parts of the array.

$15 \times 12 = ?$

The array is divided into 4 smaller arrays: $(5 \times 5) + (5 \times 10) + (7 \times 5) + (7 \times 10)$.

Step 2 Fill in the top row and left column. Here, 15 is the sum of 5 and 10, and 12 is the sum of 5 and 7.

×	5	10	15
5			
7			
12			

Step 3 Fill in each number shown in blue by multiplying the shaded numbers in its row and column. Fill in each number shown in gray by adding the blue numbers in its row or column.

×	5	10	15
5	25	50	75
7	35	70	105
12	60	120	180

Notice that there are two sets of numbers that add to 180.

$15 \times 12 = 180$

✔ Check for Understanding

Copy the chart and fill in the missing parts.

1 $14 \times 13 =$

×	4	10	■
8	■	■	■
5	■	■	■
■	■	■	■

2 $18 \times 16 =$

×	9	9	■
10	■	■	■
6	■	■	■
■	■	■	■

EXPLORE
Multiplication Records

$$25 \times 33 = ?$$

1 Find the product using any method you choose. You can use Activity Master 56: **Multiplication Tools** if you want to use an area model or chart to solve the problem.

---

2 Here is the beginning of one student's work:

```
    2 5
×   3 3
─────────
  6 0 0
  1 5 0
    6 0
    1 5
```

Can you find the numbers **600**, **150**, **60**, and **15** in your solution? Where did 600, 150, 60, and 15 come from?

REVIEW MODEL
Recording Your Process of Multiplication

You can record your steps in multiplying multi-digit numbers in a vertical format. $45 \times 36 =$

Step ①

Divide each factor into the sum of two numbers: the largest possible multiple of 10 and a one-digit number.

$45 = \boxed{40} + \boxed{5}$

$36 = \boxed{30} + \boxed{6}$

Step ②

Fill in the partial products.

$$\begin{array}{r} 45 \\ \times\ 36 \\ \hline \end{array}$$

$6 \times 40 \rightarrow \boxed{240}$

$6 \times 5 \rightarrow \boxed{30}$

$30 \times 40 \rightarrow \boxed{1,200}$

$30 \times 5 \rightarrow \boxed{150}$

Step ③

Add the partial products.

$$\begin{array}{r} 45 \\ \times\ 36 \\ \hline \end{array}$$

$40 \times 6 \rightarrow \boxed{240}$

$5 \times 6 \rightarrow \boxed{30}$

$30 \times 40 \rightarrow \boxed{1,200}$

$30 \times 5 \rightarrow \boxed{150}$

$\boxed{1,620}$

✔Check for Understanding

Calculate each product.

❶ $26 \times 17 =$

$$\begin{array}{r} 26 \\ \times\ 17 \\ \hline \boxed{\ \blacksquare\ } \\ \boxed{\ \blacksquare\ } \\ \boxed{\ \blacksquare\ } \\ \boxed{\ \blacksquare\ } \\ \boxed{\ \blacksquare\ } \end{array}$$

❷ $32 \times 48 =$

$$\begin{array}{r} 32 \\ \times\ 48 \\ \hline \boxed{\ \blacksquare\ } \\ \boxed{\ \blacksquare\ } \\ \boxed{\ \blacksquare\ } \\ \boxed{\ \blacksquare\ } \\ \boxed{\ \blacksquare\ } \end{array}$$

EXPLORE
Using Multiplication

> Read each problem and decide whether you would use multiplication to answer the question. If you would not use multiplication, what operation would you use? Then solve the problems.

1 Nina has **6 pairs of pants** and **8 different shirts**. How many different outfits can she make with her clothes?

■ outfits

---

2 Eric is putting all **36 of his shirts** into **4 drawers**. He puts the same number of shirts in each drawer. How many shirts will he put in each drawer?

■ shirts

---

3 The doctor told Paul that he is **5 feet and 6 inches** tall. Paul wanted to sound taller, so he figured out his height in inches. How many inches tall is Paul?

12 inches = 1 foot

■ inches

---

4 There are **659 students** in a school. The principal orders **1 apple** for each student. Apples are sold in baskets of **6 for 85¢**. How much will this order cost?

$ ■

REVIEW MODEL
Problem Solving Strategy
Guess and Check

The sum of two numbers is 22 and their product is 121. What are the two numbers?

Strategy: Guess and Check

Read to Understand

What do you know from reading the problem?

The sum of the two numbers is 22 and their product is 121

What do you need to find out?

What are the two numbers?

Plan

How can you solve this problem?

Think about the strategies you might use. You can guess and check.

Solve

How can you use the strategy guess and check to help solve this problem?

Guess two numbers that have a sum of 22 and check to see if their product is 121.

Check

Look back at the problem. Did you answer the questions that were asked? Does the answer make sense?

Problem Solving Practice

Use the strategy *guess and check* to solve.

1 Find the missing digits in the following multiplication problem.

$$
\begin{array}{r}
1 \ \blacksquare \ 4 \\
\times \quad \ \blacksquare \\
\hline
\blacksquare \ 6 \ 8
\end{array}
$$

2 Jayme saved $215 during the months of January and February. She saved $35 more in January than she did in February. How much money did she save in each of the two months?

Problem Solving Strategies

✔ Act It Out

✔ Draw a Picture

✔ **Guess and Check**

✔ Look for a Pattern

✔ Make a Graph

✔ Make a Model

✔ Make an Organized List

✔ Make a Table

✔ Solve a Simpler Problem

✔ Use Logical Reasoning

✔ Work Backward

✔ Write an Equation

Mixed Strategy Practice

Use any strategy to solve. Explain.

3 When Yen wrote the number 3 on the board, she said the number 9. When she wrote 6, she said 36. When she wrote 10, she said 100. If Yen wrote 7, what would she say?

4 Casey wants to buy a new outfit for a school banquet. She has a choice of three blouses, four skirts, two pair of pants, and one pair of shoes. How many different outfits can Casey make?

5 Kellie paid $3 each for 15 picture frames and sold them for $9 each. What was Kellie's profit?

6 How many different three digit numbers can be made using some or all of the digits 2, 4, and 6?

7 Carlo had basketball practice after school for 1 hour 45 minutes. He then walked to Alex's house in 20 minutes. He played video games for 35 minutes before walking 5 minutes home. He arrived home at 6:15. What time did basketball practice start?

8 Kim needs to put a fence around her rectangular garden to keep her dog away from her plants. The garden is 15 feet long and 8 feet wide. What is the area of her garden?

Choose the best vocabulary term from Word List A for each sentence.

1 The number 70 is a(n) __?__ of 10.

2 The length of a rectangle is one __?__ of the rectangle.

3 You can use a __?__ to multiply instead of using an array, grid, or table.

4 A(n) __?__ divides a space evenly into same-size squares.

5 An arrangement of objects in rows and columns is called a(n) __?__.

6 To __?__ is to find a number that is close to an exact amount.

7 A(n) __?__ is used to display and organize information.

8 Miles, minutes, quarts, and kilograms are examples of __?__.

9 The __?__ states that multiplying a sum by a number is the same as multiplying each addend by the number and then adding the products.

Complete each analogy using the best term from Word List B.

10 Letter is to word as __?__ is to total product.

11 Accurate calculation is to "exact amount" as __?__ is to "about how many".

Word List A

array
Commutative Property
dimension
Distributive Property
estimate
grid
multiple
partial product
reasonableness
table
units
vertical format

Word List B

estimate
partial product
unit

Talk Math

Discuss with a partner what you have just learned about multiplying. Use the vocabulary terms *partial product*, *multi-digit number*, and *grid*.

12 How does splitting numbers make it easier to multiply multi-digit numbers?

13 How is using a vertical format to multiply like using a grid?

Word Definition Map

14 **Create a word definition map for the word *estimation*.**

A What is it?

B What is it like?

C What are some examples?

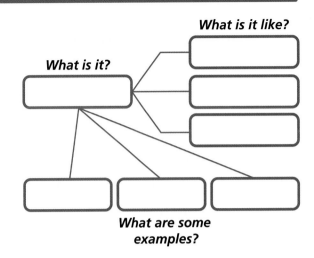

Word Web

15 **Create a word web using the term *reasonableness*.**

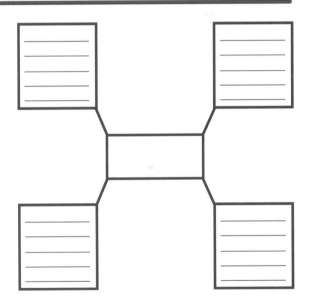

TABLE The word *table* has many uses. A *table* can be something you sit at. You could use a *table*cloth, a *table*spoon, and *table*ware. You could play *table* tennis, which is a game like tennis that is played on a table. You could find a chapter title in a *table* of contents. In math, you would use a *table* to show data in rows and columns. A math *table* makes it easier to understand data.

GAME

Find a Factor

Game Purpose
To practice multiplication facts and using fact families

Materials
- Activity Master 48: *Product Cards*
- Activity Master 49: *Factor Cards*

Find a Factor

70   35   99

How To Play The Game

1 This is a game for 4 players. Each group will need one set of Product cards and two sets of Factor Cards.

- Cut out the Product Cards. Mix them up. Put them face down in a pile.

- Cut out the Factor Cards. Mix them up. Give each player 12 cards. Everyone places their cards face up in front of them.

2 Turn over the top Product Card. All players turn face down any of their Factor Cards that are factors of that product.

Example: The Product Card is: 64

José has these Factor Cards in front of him:

6	6	2	11	8	1
9	7	3	12	2	6

José turns over all of his Factor Cards that show a factor of 64. Now his cards look like this:

6	6		11		
9	7	3	12		6

3 Turn over the next Product Card and keep playing.

4 The first player to turn all of his of her Factor Cards face down wins! Everyone should check to be sure that the winner's Factor Cards match the Product Cards.

GAME

Profitable Products

> **Game Purpose**
> To practice solving simpler problems to complete multi-digit multiplication problems
>
> **Materials**
> • Activity Master 48: *Product Cards*
> • Calculator

How To Play The Game

1 Play this game with a partner. Cut out the Product Cards. Mix them up. Put them face down in a pile.

2 Each player picks a card and turns it face up. Use the two numbers as factors in a multi-digit multiplication problem.

3 Decide who will go first.

Players take turns choosing and calculating a partial product. Each player gets 100 points plus the value of the partial product. You can check each problem with a calculator.

4 Take turns going first for each problem. The first player to score 5,000 points wins!

Example: Reena and Ken are using these Product Cards: | 42 | | 54 |

These are the partial products:

$40 \times 50 = 2,000$ $40 \times 4 = 160$ $2 \times 50 = 100$ $2 \times 4 = 8$

Reena goes first. She chooses $40 \times 50 = 2,000$. So, she gets $100 + 2,000 = 2,100$ points.

CHALLENGE

There are many ways of multiplying. Here is another way to multiply that you can try. It is called lattice multiplication.

Multiply 36 × 27.

In the grid below, the factors are at the top and on the right. Each space is filled using a multiplication fact. For example, 6 × 2 = 12, so write 12 at the upper right.

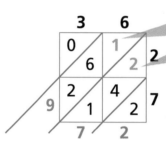

Put each digit in a separate section of the box.

Then add the numbers along the diagonal lines, starting at the bottom right. Regroup if you need to. So, you can read the product of 36 and 27: 36 × 27 = 972.

Copy each grid. Use lattice multiplication to find the product.

1 248 × 6

2 579 × 4

3 63 × 75

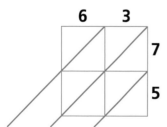

4 26 × 59

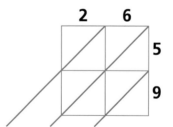

Chapter

7 Fractions

Dear Student,

Welcome to the fractions chapter! You probably have learned about fractions before, and you may have heard people around you using words like **half, quarter,** or **two thirds,** all of which are fractions.

Do you think you could explain what a quarter of a dollar means? Could you write a fraction for it?

In this chapter, you'll be learning about fractions that are **less than 1** (like one fourth) as well as fractions that are **greater than 1** (like two and a half). You'll learn lots of different names for the same fraction, and you'll figure out which of two fractions is greater and which is smaller. Along the way, you'll get to use pattern blocks, Cuisenaire® Rods, and rulers to represent various fractions.

In the pictures below, can you tell which piece is half of another piece? How can you tell?

Have fun! You're already a fraction of the way there!

Mathematically yours,
The authors of *Think Math!*

No Loafing Please!

Have you ever heard the expression "the best thing since sliced bread?" Thank Otto Frederick Rohwedde, who is called the "father of sliced bread." He worked for many years to build a machine to slice and wrap bread. The machine was first used by a baker in Michigan in 1928.

FACT·ACTIVITY 1

The identical loaves of bread to the right are sliced into different numbers of equal slices. Answer the questions using the pictures of the bread.

1 Suppose you eat 1 slice of loaf A. What part of the loaf did you eat? What part of the loaf is not eaten?

2 What part of loaf C is 1 slice? What part of the loaf is 6 slices?

3 If you eat 1 slice of loaf A and your friend eats 1 slice of loaf B, who eats the most bread? Explain.

4 Draw a round loaf of bread. Divide it into 8 equal pieces. Shade the pieces to show a fraction greater than $\frac{1}{4}$ and less than $\frac{1}{2}$.

Loaf A

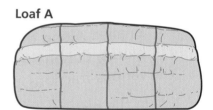

Loaf B

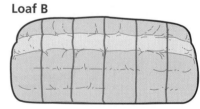

Loaf C

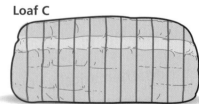

Bread is an important food in many cultures. It comes in all sizes, shapes, and forms. Gingerbread is a sweet bread that came from countries in Europe.

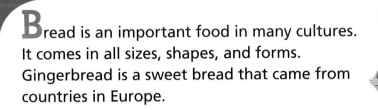

The "gingerbread man" to the right is cut into 30 equal squares. Use the figure to answer the questions. Copy the figure onto grid paper and use shading to help.

❶ How many pieces make up $\frac{1}{10}$ of the figure?

❷ John eats the pieces of the gingerbread that make up the head. What part of the gingerbread does he eat?

❸ Nikki eats the pieces that make up the legs. Write a fraction addition sentence to find the part of the gingerbread that she eats.

❹ Write a word problem involving addition of fractions that can be answered by using the gingerbread figure. Give your problem to a classmate to solve.

CHAPTER PROJECT

Find a recipe for making bread. Select a recipe that has at least two fractional ingredients, such as $\frac{1}{4}$ cup oil. Copy the fraction amounts.

- Make a table that shows how much of those ingredients you will need to make 1 bread, 2 breads, 3 breads, and so on, up to 6 breads.

- Find a classmate whose recipe uses one of the same ingredients. Write a comparison of the fractions of the amounts needed for making 1 loaf of bread.

The longest loaf of bread measured in the U.S. was 2,356 feet. It was baked in 1977.

EXPLORE
Exploring Fractions With Pattern Blocks

Use pattern blocks like these to answer these questions.

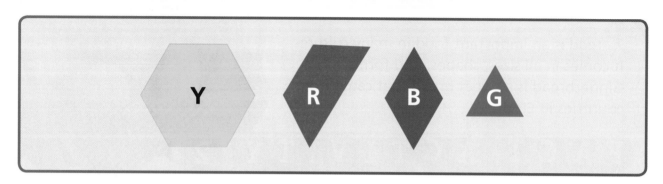

1 If R is 1, then what is Y ?

2 If Y is 1, then what is R ?

3 If Y is 1, then what is B ?

4 If B is 1, then what is G ?

5 If G is 1, then what is R ?

6 If R is 1, then what is GGG ?

7 If R is 1, then what is GGG ?

8 If B is 1, then what is R ?

REVIEW MODEL
Using Pattern Blocks to Show Fractions

You can use pattern blocks to model fractions.

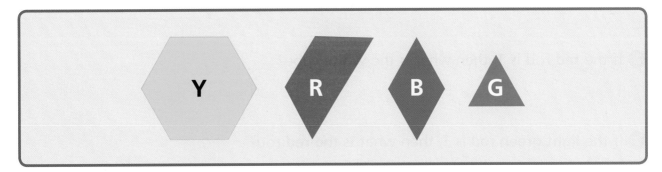

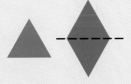

2 triangles match 1 rhombus.
So, 1 triangle is $\frac{1}{2}$ of a rhombus.

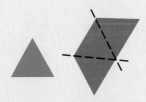

3 triangles match 1 trapezoid.
So, 1 triangle is $\frac{1}{3}$ of a trapezoid,
and 2 triangles are $\frac{2}{3}$ of a trapezoid.

6 triangles match 1 hexagon. So,
1 triangle is $\frac{1}{6}$ of a hexagon, and
3 triangles are $\frac{3}{6}$, or $\frac{1}{2}$, of a hexagon.

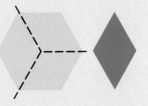

3 rhombuses match 1 hexagon.
So, 1 rhombus is $\frac{1}{3}$ of a hexagon,
and 2 rhombuses are $\frac{2}{3}$ of a hexagon.

✔Check for Understanding

Solve.

❶ How many trapezoids match one hexagon?

❷ What fraction of the hexagon is one trapezoid?

❸ How many triangles match one hexagon?

EXPLORE
What is the Whole?

Use Cuisenaire® Rods to answer these questions.

1 If the **white** cube is 1, then what is the **red** rod?

2 If the **red** rod is 1, then what is the **white** cube?

3 If the **light green** rod is 1, then what is the **red** rod?

4 If the **light green** rod is 1, then what is the **purple** rod?

5 If the **purple** rod is 1, then what is the **red** rod?

6 If the **purple** rod is 1, then what is the **yellow** rod?

7 If the **purple** rod is 1, then what is the **dark green** rod?

8 If the **blue** rod is 1, then what is the **white** cube?

9 If the **blue** rod is 1, then what is the **black** rod?

10 If the **brown** rod is 1, then what is the **orange** rod?

REVIEW MODEL
Using Cuisenaire® Rods

Activity 1 **The value of the light green rod, G, is $\frac{1}{2}$. The value of the blue rod, E, can be found by using the light green rod.**

Step ❶

Compare the **lengths** of the rods.

G		

E

The blue rod is **3** times as long as the light green rod.

Step ❷

There are 3 rods, each worth $\frac{1}{2}$.

G $= \frac{1}{2}$

E

So, the value of the blue rod is $\frac{3}{2}$, or $1\frac{1}{2}$.

Activity 2 **The value of the brown rod, N, is $\frac{4}{5}$. The value of the purple rod, P, can be found by using the brown rod.**

Step ❶

Compare the **lengths** of the rods.

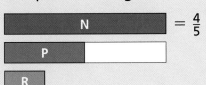

N $= \frac{4}{5}$

P

R

The brown rod is 4 times as long as the red rod. The purple rod is twice as long as the red rod.

Step ❷

Use the **value** of the red rod to find the value of the purple rod.

N $\qquad \frac{4}{5} = \frac{2}{5} + \frac{2}{5}$

P $\qquad \frac{1}{2}$ of $\frac{4}{5} = \frac{2}{5}$

R

The red rod is $\frac{1}{5}$ because 4 red rods is $\frac{4}{5}$. Two red rods is $\frac{2}{5}$, so the value of the purple rod is $\frac{2}{5}$.

✔ Check for Understanding

Find the value of the bottom rod.

❶

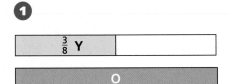

❷

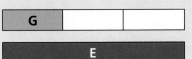

❸

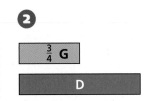

EXPLORE
Finding One Half

You might sketch this rectangle on a piece of scratch paper to help you answer these questions.

1 Imagine that the rectangle is divided into **4 equal pieces.** How many pieces would equal $\frac{1}{2}$ of the rectangle?

2 Imagine that the rectangle is divided into **10 equal pieces.** How many pieces would equal $\frac{1}{2}$ of the rectangle?

3 Imagine that the rectangle is divided into **20 equal pieces.** How many pieces would equal $\frac{1}{2}$ of the rectangle?

4 Imagine that the rectangle is divided into **100 equal pieces.** How many pieces would equal $\frac{1}{2}$ of the rectangle?

5 How did you figure out the number of pieces in $\frac{1}{2}$ of the rectangle?

EXPLORE
Comparing Fractions

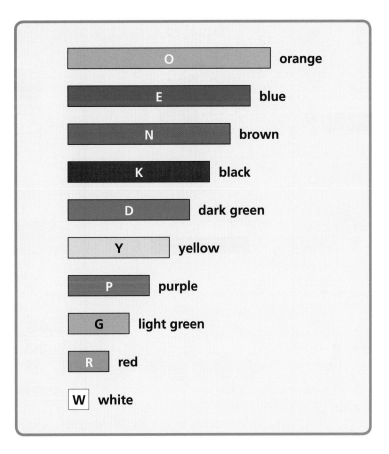

1 Which rod is $\frac{1}{2}$ of the **orange** rod?

2 Which rod is $\frac{1}{5}$ of the **orange** rod?

3 Which is greater, $\frac{1}{2}$ or $\frac{1}{5}$?

4 Which rod is $\frac{1}{2}$ of the **brown** rod?

5 Which rod is $\frac{1}{4}$ of the **brown** rod?

6 Which is greater, $\frac{1}{2}$ or $\frac{1}{4}$?

7 Which rod is $\frac{1}{3}$ of the **blue** rod?

8 Which rod is $\frac{1}{9}$ of the **blue** rod?

9 Which is greater, $\frac{1}{3}$ or $\frac{1}{9}$?

REVIEW MODEL
Comparing Fractions to $\frac{1}{2}$

Less than $\frac{1}{2}$	Equal to $\frac{1}{2}$	Greater than $\frac{1}{2}$
$\frac{2}{10}$	$\frac{2}{4}$	$\frac{51}{100}$
$\frac{1}{3}$	$\frac{3}{6}$	$\frac{4}{5}$
$\frac{8}{17}$	$\frac{5}{10}$	$\frac{9}{12}$
Top number is less than half of the bottom number.	Top number is exactly half of the bottom number.	Top number is greater than half of the bottom number.

✔Check for Understanding

Compare the fraction to $\frac{1}{2}$. On a separate sheet of paper, write <, =, or >.

1 $\frac{2}{6} \bullet \frac{1}{2}$

2 $\frac{3}{5} \bullet \frac{1}{2}$

3 $\frac{4}{10} \bullet \frac{1}{2}$

4 $\frac{9}{18} \bullet \frac{1}{2}$

5 $\frac{5}{12} \bullet \frac{1}{2}$

6 $\frac{4}{8} \bullet \frac{1}{2}$

7 $\frac{15}{24} \bullet \frac{1}{2}$

8 $\frac{25}{80} \bullet \frac{1}{2}$

9 $\frac{23}{35} \bullet \frac{1}{2}$

REVIEW MODEL
Finding Equivalent Fractions Using Models

You can find the fraction of a model that is shaded.

number of shaded pieces = 1

total number of pieces = 2

fraction shaded = $\dfrac{\text{number of shaded pieces}}{\text{total number of pieces}}$

fraction shaded = $\dfrac{1}{2}$

number of shaded pieces = 3

total number of pieces = 6

fraction shaded = $\dfrac{\text{number of shaded pieces}}{\text{total number of pieces}}$

fraction shaded = $\dfrac{3}{6}$

The same portion of each rectangle is shaded, so $\dfrac{1}{2}$ and $\dfrac{3}{6}$ are equivalent.

number of shaded pieces = 10

total number of pieces = 15

fraction shaded = $\dfrac{10}{15}$

number of shaded pieces = 2

total number of pieces = 3

fraction shaded = $\dfrac{2}{3}$

The same portion of each rectangle is shaded, so $\dfrac{2}{3}$ and $\dfrac{10}{15}$ are equivalent.

✔ Check for Understanding

Find the equivalent fractions shown by the models.

1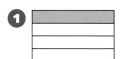

$\dfrac{\blacksquare}{\blacksquare} = \dfrac{\blacksquare}{\blacksquare}$

2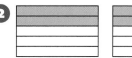

$\dfrac{\blacksquare}{\blacksquare} = \dfrac{\blacksquare}{\blacksquare}$

3

$\dfrac{\blacksquare}{\blacksquare} = \dfrac{\blacksquare}{\blacksquare}$

4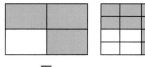

$\dfrac{\blacksquare}{\blacksquare} = \dfrac{\blacksquare}{\blacksquare}$

EXPLORE
Measuring Lengths

Use this measuring tape to find the lengths of the pieces of string.

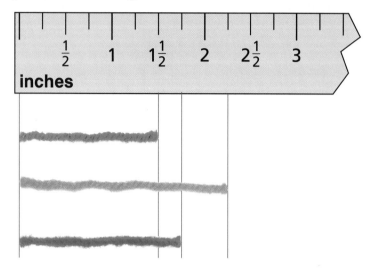

Record the lengths of these lines.

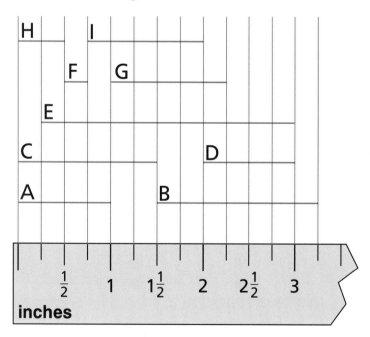

REVIEW MODEL
Finding the Length of a Line

You can use an inch-ruler to find how long a line is.

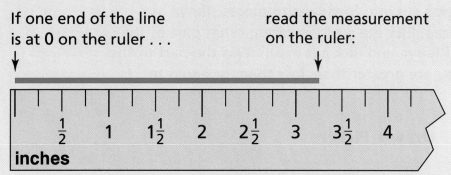

If one end of the line is at 0 on the ruler . . .

read the measurement on the ruler:

The line is $3\frac{1}{4}$ inches long.

If one end of the line is **not** at 0 on the ruler, count by quarter inches from the beginning to the end of the line.

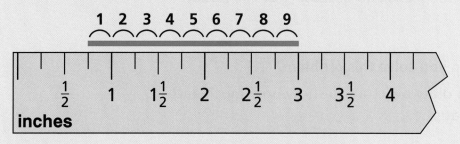

The line is 9 quarter inches long. Since there are 4 quarter inches in 1 inch, the line is $2\frac{1}{4}$ inches long.

✔ Check for Understanding

Find the length of the line.

1

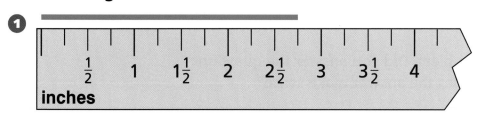

2

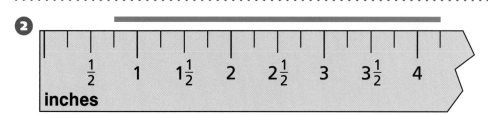

REVIEW MODEL
Problem Solving Strategy
Draw a Picture

A pizza was cut into 8 equal-size pieces. Tanya ate $\frac{1}{4}$ of the pizza. Rick ate $\frac{3}{8}$ of the pizza. What part of the pizza did Tanya and Rick eat in all? Was the part of the pizza they ate greater than, less than, or equal to $\frac{1}{2}$?

Strategy: Draw a Picture

Read to Understand

What do you know from reading the problem?

The pizza was cut into 8 equal-size pieces. Tanya ate $\frac{1}{4}$ of the pizza and Rick ate $\frac{3}{8}$ of the pizza.

Plan

How can you solve this problem?

You can draw a picture to show how much each person ate.

Solve

How can you draw a picture of the problem?

Draw and divide a circle into 8 equal parts to represent the cut pizza. Shade $\frac{1}{4}$ to represent Tanya's part and $\frac{3}{8}$ to represent Rick's part. More than half the circle is shaded, so they ate more than $\frac{1}{2}$.

Check

Look back at the problem. Did you answer the questions that were asked? Does the answer make sense?

Problem Solving Practice

Draw a picture to solve.

① Juan spent $\frac{2}{5}$ hour mowing his lawn and $\frac{1}{2}$ hour practicing the piano. Which activity did he spend more time on?

② Kyle used toothpicks to form some triangles and quadrilaterals on his desk. He used 22 toothpicks to make 6 figures. How many triangles and how many quadrilaterals did he make?

Problem Solving Strategies

- ✔ Act It Out
- ✔ **Draw a Picture**
- ✔ Guess and Check
- ✔ Look for a Pattern
- ✔ Make a Graph
- ✔ Make a Model
- ✔ Make an Organized List
- ✔ Make a Table
- ✔ Solve a Simpler Problem
- ✔ Use Logical Reasoning
- ✔ Work Backward
- ✔ Write an Equation

Mixed Strategy Practice

Use any strategy to solve. Explain.

③ Kari built a low brick wall along the side of her house. The wall is 30 bricks wide. Each brick in the wall is 8 inches wide. How many feet wide is the wall?

④ Jeff spent $12.00 for a pizza and two drinks. The pizza costs twice as much as the two drinks. How much did each item cost?

For 5–6, use the yard-sale chart.

Yard Sale	
Item	Price
Books	$0.50
Toy trucks and cars	$0.75
Games	$0.25

⑤ Jake bought 2 books and 4 games. How much change did he get from $10.00?

⑥ Anne bought 1 truck, 1 car, and 3 books. Scott bought 4 books. How much more did Anne spend than Scott?

⑦ A rectangle is made from a 6 in. × 6 in. square and an 8 in. × 6 in. rectangle. What is the perimeter of the large rectangle?

⑧ John is 5 years older than his brother. The product of their ages is 36. How old is John?

Choose the best vocabulary term from Word List A for each sentence.

1 The symbol < means ___?___ .

2 The ___?___ tells the number of equal parts in the whole.

3 The ___?___ is the top number in a fraction.

4 Three inches is one ___?___ of a foot.

5 To read $\frac{1}{2} = \frac{3}{6}$, you say "one half ___?___ three sixths."

6 The symbols <, >, and = are used to ___?___ numbers.

7 A(n) ___?___ is a number that can represent a part of a whole.

8 When you ___?___ 4 and 7, the result is 11.

9 If two fractions name the same value, then they are ___?___ .

10 The symbol > means ___?___ .

Word List A

add
compare
denominator
distance
eighth
equal
equivalent
fourth
fraction
greater than
greatest
is equal to
least
length
less than
numerator

Complete each analogy using the best term from Word List B.

11 Equal is to = as ___?___ is to >.

12 Four is to whole number as one fourth is to ___?___ .

13 Two is to half as five is to ___?___ .

Word List B

combine
fifth
fraction
greater than
less than
ninth

Talk Math

Discuss with a partner what you have learned about fractions. Use the vocabulary terms *denominator*, *fraction*, and *numerator*.

14 How can you compare a fraction to $\frac{1}{2}$?

15 How can you tell whether two fractions are equivalent?

16 How can you order fractions from least to greatest?

Word Definition Map

17 **Create a word definition map for the word *fraction*.**

A What is it?

B What is it like?

C What are some examples?

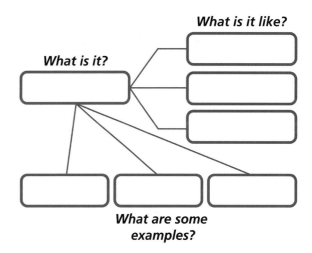

Word Line

18 **Create a word line using the words *eighth, fifth, fourth, ninth, seventh, sixth,* and *tenth*.**

Words:

Sequence:

_____

What's in a Word?

FRACTION In everyday language, the word *fraction* might not be a specific amount. "A *fraction*" could mean "some" or "part" or "not all." If someone says "I paid a *fraction* of the price," you know that the person paid less than full price—but you don't know exactly how much less.

In math, a *fraction* is a specific number. A fraction tells exactly how many parts there are and how many of those parts are being used. If someone says "I paid half price," the person is talking about a specific *fraction* of the price, $\frac{1}{2}$.

GAME

Where is $\frac{1}{2}$?

Game Purpose

To practice comparing fractions with $\frac{1}{2}$

Materials

• Activity Masters 61 and 62 (*Fraction Cards*)

• Cuisenaire® Rods

How To Play The Game

 Play this game with a partner. Cut out the *Fraction Cards* from Activity Masters 61 and 62. Decide who will be Player 1 and who will be Player 2.

• Mix up the cards.

• Place them in a pile face down between you.

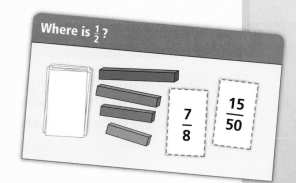

Where is $\frac{1}{2}$?

Player 1 and Player 2 each pick one card from the pile.

• Compare your fraction to $\frac{1}{2}$. You can use Cuisenaire® Rods.

• Follow the chart to see which player keeps both cards.

How the Fractions Compare	Who Keeps the Cards
Both fractions are greater than $\frac{1}{2}$.	Player 1
Both fractions are less than $\frac{1}{2}$.	Player 1
One fraction is greater than $\frac{1}{2}$. The other fraction is less than $\frac{1}{2}$.	Player 2

Continue playing until all the *Fraction Cards* are gone.

The player with more cards at the end of the game wins.

Fraction Least to Greatest

Game Purpose
To practice comparing fractions

Materials
- Activity Masters 66 and 67 (*Fraction Cards*)
- Stopwatch or clock with a second hand

Fraction Least to Greatest

How To Play The Game

1 This is a game for two players. The object of the game is to place the fraction cards in order. Decide who will be the Placer. The other player will be the Timer.

2 The Placer mixes up all the Fraction Cards and arranges them in a stack.

3 When the Timer says to start, the Placer turns over one card at a time and makes a row of cards with the fractions in order from least to greatest.

4 The Timer stops play at the end of **60** seconds.
- The Timer checks the order of the cards.
- If the Timer finds an error, the Placer may remove one or more cards to correct the line of cards. The Placer may not rearrange the cards.
- The Placer gets 1 point for each card in the line.

5 Switch roles, and play again. The first player to reach 50 points wins.

CHALLENGE

A tangram is a Chinese puzzle square cut into 7 different shapes and sizes. Tangrams are usually made from plastic or cardboard. Suppose you could buy a tangram-shaped candy bar. You could buy the whole tangram. Or you could buy each piece separately.

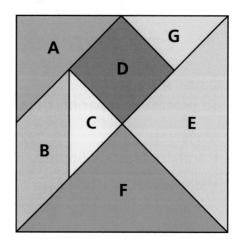

If the piece labeled F were to sell for $1.00, what would be the cost of each of the other pieces?

- Piece E would also cost $1.00 because pieces E and F are congruent.

- Piece A would cost $0.50 because piece A is $\frac{1}{2}$ of piece F.

- Pieces C and G would each cost $0.25 because each of them is $\frac{1}{4}$ of piece F.

- Pieces B and D would each cost $0.50, the same as piece A. All 3 pieces have the same area.

Use the tangram model above to solve each problem.

What would each of the other pieces cost:

1 if piece D cost $1.00?

2 if piece A cost $0.50?

3 if piece B cost $0.30?

4 if piece F cost $2.40?

5 if pieces A and D together cost $2.00?

Dear Student,

In this chapter, you'll be zooming in on the number line. Can you think of a number that is between 10 and 20 on the number line? How about a number that's between 1 and 2 on the number line?

You'll be seeing numbers like 3.25 and 98.6 when you zoom in on the number line. Have you seen numbers like this before? If so, where have you seen them?

Before you get started, though, you'll be looking at really big numbers like 9,638,702. What number is this? By reviewing some of the rules we use to write big numbers like this one, you will start to have ideas of what the digits to the right of the "." in the numbers 3.25 and 98.6 mean.

For the millionth time, enjoy!

Mathematically yours,
The authors of *Think Math!*

Ready, Set, Down the Hill

Every year since 1934, tens of thousands of people flock to Derby Down in Akron, Ohio, to watch the Soap Box Derby Championships. In home-built "cars" youths from age 8 through age 17 race down a hill depending only on gravity for power. Each racer's run is over in less than 30 seconds.

In a typical Soap Box Derby, cars cannot have a motor, but must have at least four wheels and brakes. The driver must wear a helmet. Spending to make the car is limited to a certain amount.

FACT·ACTIVITY 1

1 The estimated population of Akron, Ohio, in 2005 was 210,795. Write the estimated population in expanded form.

2 Find the population of the city or town where you live. Is it greater than or less than the population of Akron?

3 Competitors from the U.S. and from other countries travel to Akron for the Soap Box Derby Championships. The table shows the distances from some cities to Akron. List the cities in order from least to greatest distance from Akron.

Distance From Some Cities To Akron, Ohio	
City	**Miles**
Juneau, AK	2,780
Milford, CT	991
Montreal, Canada	1,152
Salem, OR	2,096
San Juan, Puerto Rico	1,668
San Diego, CA	2,036

4 Corey is traveling from Miami, Florida, to be in the Soap Box Derby Championship. Miami is 1,061 miles from Akron. Between which two distances in the chart is 1,061 miles?

FACT · ACTIVITY 2

Soap Box Derby racers compete as teams. An adult helps the child build the soap box car and local businesses might help too. The table at the right shows the times of some winners.

Use the table to answer the questions.

1 Which team had the fastest time? Explain.

2 What is the difference between Wargo's time and Kimball's time?

3 Up until 1964, stopwatches only recorded winning times to 1 decimal place. What would Pearson and Wargo's times be if they were only rounded to tenths?

4 How would you write Pearson's time as a mixed number?

CHAPTER PROJECT

Materials:
stopwatch (with hundredths of a second accuracy); wooden board (to use as ramp); 9 textbooks, close to the same thickness; tennis ball (or any ball that will roll across the classroom floor)

Build a ramp using a board and a textbook as shown. Rest one end of the ramp against the book and the other end on the floor near the wall. Roll the ball down the ramp. Record the time it takes to roll from the top of the ramp (start) to the wall (finish). Repeat four times, each time adding 2 more books.

- When you add more books to the ramp, does the recorded time increase or decrease?

- Which ramp produced the fastest time?

- Find the difference in time for each time you rolled the ball down the ramp.

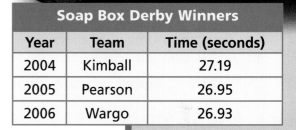

Soap Box Derby Winners		
Year	Team	Time (seconds)
2004	Kimball	27.19
2005	Pearson	26.95
2006	Wargo	26.93

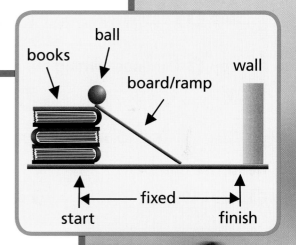

REVIEW MODEL
Reading and Writing Numbers

You can use a place-value chart to read and write whole numbers.

Read the number 2,407,695.

Step ❶ Fill in the digits in the chart, starting at the right.

Hundred Millions | Ten Millions | One Millions | Hundred Thousands | Ten Thousands | One Thousands | Hundreds | Tens | Ones

2,4 0 7,6 9 5

Step ❷ Read
the number of millions, ⟶ two *million,*
then the number of thousands, ⟶ four hundred seven *thousand,*
then the number of ones. ⟶ six hundred ninety-five

Write the number six million, five hundred eighty-one thousand, four hundred nine.

Step ❶ Write the number of millions. ⟶ 6

Step ❷ Continue, writing the number of thousands. ⟶ 6,581

Step ❸ Continue, writing the number of ones. ⟶ 6,581,409

✔ Check for Understanding

Read the number.

❶ 5,231,699

❷ 3,074,501

❸ 260,008

On a separate sheet of paper, write the number.

❹ nine million, one hundred eight thousand, three hundred fourteen

❺ six million, two thousand, nine hundred sixty

❻ four hundred twenty-two thousand, thirty-eight

REVIEW MODEL
Understanding Decimals

You have already learned that fractions are numbers that are *between* whole numbers on a number line.

Decimals are another way of writing fractions. Like fractions, decimals are found between whole numbers on a number line.

Decimals between 1 and 2 are here.

Decimals between 2 and 3 are here.

Decimals between 3 and 4 are here.

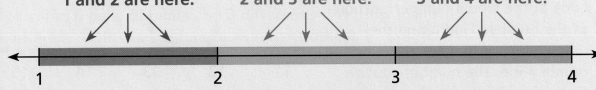

A decimal has one or more digits to the right of the decimal point. One way to read a decimal is to read left-to-right, inserting the word "point" for the decimal point. (You will learn more precise ways of reading decimals in later lessons.)

Decimal	Read
5.7	"five point seven"
12.39	"twelve point three nine" OR "twelve point thirty-nine"
0.4	"zero point four"

To input a decimal on a calculator, press the decimal point key for the decimal point.

To input 8.45, press

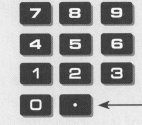

✔ Check for Understanding

Name the two whole numbers between which the decimal lies.

1 2.5

2 13.711

3 0.9

State how you would read the decimal.

4 1.2

5 20.4

6 6.17

7 Explain how you would input the number 92.05 on a calculator.

REVIEW MODEL
Placing Decimals

You can use the digits in a decimal number to decide where to place the number on the number line.

Place 12.74 on the number line.

Step 1

Look at the whole-number portion of the number. Find it and the whole number that follows it on the number line. The number you are looking for lies somewhere between the two whole numbers.

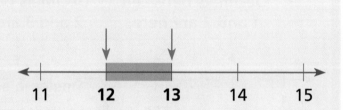

Step 2

Focus on the part of the number line between the two whole numbers. Find the tenths digit of the number and the tenths digit that follows it on the number line. The number you are looking for lies somewhere between the two tenths digits.

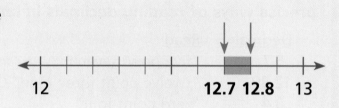

Step 3

Focus on the part of the number line between the two tenths digits. Think of it as being divided into 10 equal parts, numbered 1 to 10. Find the hundredths digit of the number and mark the point.

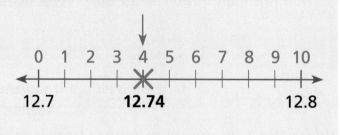

✓ Check for Understanding

Draw a number line from 5 to 8. Mark it in tenths. Then mark and label each point on the number line.

1 5.73

2 7.19

3 6.05

EXPLORE
Comparing Fractions and Decimals

For each pair of numbers, decide which is larger. Then, on a separate sheet of paper, use words, pictures, or numbers to tell how you know.

1 0.5 and $\frac{3}{4}$

2 13.7 and $13\frac{4}{10}$

3 4.1 and $4\frac{7}{10}$

4 42.4 and $42\frac{3}{10}$

REVIEW MODEL
Comparing Fractions with Decimals

You can use a common benchmark or a number line to compare a fraction with a decimal.

Compare 6.8 and $6\frac{3}{10}$.

One Way ·

- Compare both numbers to the same number (called a benchmark). Here, compare both numbers to $6\frac{1}{2}$. (Remember: $\frac{1}{2} = \frac{5}{10}$.)

  $6.8 = 6\frac{8}{10}$. Since $\frac{8}{10}$ is larger than $\frac{5}{10}$, 6.8 is larger than $6\frac{1}{2}$.

  Since $\frac{3}{10}$ is smaller than $\frac{5}{10}$, $6\frac{3}{10}$ is smaller than $6\frac{1}{2}$.

  So, 6.8 is larger than $6\frac{3}{10}$.

Another Way ·

- Place both numbers on a number line. The number farther to the right is larger.

6       $6\frac{3}{10}$ 6.8   7

6.8 is larger than $6\frac{3}{10}$.

✔Check for Understanding

Which number is larger?

1 2.1 or $2\frac{9}{10}$

2 $6\frac{3}{10}$ or 5.9

3 1.4 or $1\frac{7}{10}$

4 $9\frac{1}{2}$ or 9.9

5 4.6 or $4\frac{4}{10}$

6 $8\frac{1}{4}$ or 8.6

EXPLORE
Representing Decimals with Blocks

You've probably worked with blocks like these before:

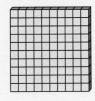

For this activity, a flat has a value of 1.

1 What decimal shows the value of 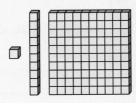 ?

_____

2 What decimal shows the value of ▱ ?

_____

3 What decimal shows the value of these blocks?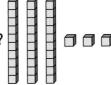

_____

4 Use base-ten blocks to represent 1.23.

_____

5 How can base-ten blocks help you solve this problem: 1.23 + 1.45?

_____

6 Mr. Guttman's class is having a party and they're buying cheese to make sandwiches. They buy 1.23 pounds of cheddar cheese and 1.45 pounds of American cheese. How many pounds of cheese do they buy?

_____

7 What is 1.23 + 1.45 + 1.00?

_____

8 What is 1.23 + 1.45 + 0.10?

_____

9 What is 1.23 + 1.45 + 0.01?

EXPLORE
Adding Decimals with Blocks

Once again, has a value of 1.

Use base-ten blocks to represent this problem and find the answer.

1 Naomi wore a pedometer to find out how far she walked each day. On Monday, she walked 1.18 miles home from school and then 0.16 miles to her friend Jennifer's house. How far did she walk on Monday?

1.18   +   0.16   =   ■

Use base-ten blocks to represent and answer these problems.

2 Jill wanted to know whether she had enough birdseed in her 1-pound box to fill her two birdfeeders. She knew that one birdfeeder used 0.46 pounds of seed and the other used 0.37 pounds. How much birdseed does she need? Will she have enough?

0.46   +   0.37   =   ■

3 Serena needs school supplies. She bought a notebook that cost $1.64 and a pencil that cost $0.53. How much money did she spend on supplies?

1.64   +   0.53   =   ■

4 Aki and Chris had a contest to see who could make the longest line of dominoes in one minute. Aki won with a line that was 0.42 meters long. Chris's line was 0.28 meters. Chris decided to finish building her line so it would be as long as Aki's. How much longer does it need to be?

0.28   +   ■   =   0.42

EXPLORE
Subtracting Decimals with Blocks

Once again, has a value of 1.

Drawings show how students might complete the problem

1 Represent this problem with base-ten blocks.

0.71 — **0.45** = ■

---

2 What is the difference between 0.71 and 0.45?

Use base-ten blocks to represent and complete these subtraction sentences.

3 0.83 — 0.37 = ■

4 1.24 — 0.52 = ■

5 1.03 — ■ = 0.85

REVIEW MODEL
Problem Solving Strategy
Act It Out

> On his first try, Cory high-jumped 1.1 meters. On his second try, he high-jumped 0.94 meters. How much higher did he jump on his first try than he did on his second?

Strategy: Act it Out

Read to Understand

What do you know from reading the problem?

Cory high-jumped twice. He made 1.1 meters on his first try and 0.94 meters on his second try.

What do you need to find out?

the difference between the heights

Plan

How can you solve this problem?

You could *act it out* using base-ten blocks.

Solve

How can you find the difference between the two heights?

Use base-ten blocks to model 1.1. Exchange one rod for 10 cubes. Remove 9 rods and 4 cubes, representing 0.94. The difference is 0.16.

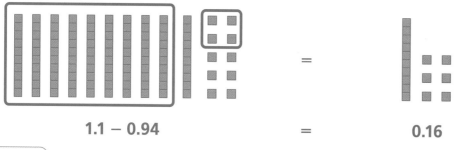

$$1.1 - 0.94 \qquad = \qquad 0.16$$

Check

Look back at the problem. Did you answer the questions that were asked? Does the answer make sense?

Yes; to check if the answer makes sense, I can add 0.16 + 0.94 and see if the sum is 1.1.

Problem Solving Practice

Problem Solving Strategies

✔ **Act It Out**
✔ Draw a Picture
✔ Guess and Check
✔ Look for a Pattern
✔ Make a Graph
✔ Make a Model
✔ Make an Organized List
✔ Make a Table
✔ Solve a Simpler Problem
✔ Use Logical Reasoning
✔ Work Backward
✔ Write an Equation

Use the strategy *act it out* to solve.

1 The shaded figure below is made of three congruent squares. How can the shaded figure be divided into four congruent figures?

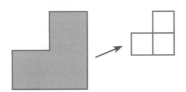

2 Six students went to a meeting. Each student shook hands with each of the other students once. How many handshakes were exchanged?

Mixed Strategy Practice

Use any strategy to solve.

3 There are 16 rows of seats in the West Side Theater. Each row has 12 seats. Tickets to a play cost $5. If all the seats are sold, how much money will the theater owner make?

4 Joanie rode her bike at a rate of 8 miles per hour for 3 hours. She wants to ride 50 miles. How much farther does she have to ride?

5 Al is 10 years older than Bob. Carl is 10 years younger than Dave. Dave is 30 years older than Bob. List the four is order from oldest to youngest.

6 The figure below is made from 18 toothpicks. Which two toothpicks can you remove so that exactly four squares remain?

7 If you take Glen's age, multiply it by 2, add 16, and divide by 5, you get his brother's age. Glen's brother is 6. How old is Glen?

8 Mr. Babbitt made two telephone calls. The calls lasted a total of 44 minutes. If one call lasted 6 minutes more than the other, how long did the longest call last?

Vocabulary

Choose the best vocabulary term from Word List A for each sentence.

1 The ___?___ is the number in a fraction that is below the bar.

2 ___?___ are symbols, such as 0, 1, 2, 3, 4, 5, 6, 7, 8, and 9, that are used to write numbers.

3 The answer to an addition problem is called a(n) ___?___.

4 In ___?___ the cents are written as a decimal part of a dollar.

5 The value of a digit in a number is determined by its ___?___.

6 The ___?___ between two cities is how far you have to travel to get from one city to the other.

7 Pennies tell how many ___?___ of a dollar there are.

8 The set of ___?___ starts at 0 and goes up one unit at a time without end.

Word List A

base-10 system
denominator
diagram
digits
distance
dollar notation
hundredths
meter stick
metric system
non-decimal
  portion
numerator
place value
sum
tenths
whole numbers

Complete each analogy using the best term from Word List B.

9 Letters are to words as ___?___ are to numbers.

10 Dollar is to dimes as one is to ___?___.

Word List B

decimal
  portion
digits
grid
place value
point
tenths

Talk Math

Discuss with a partner what you have just learned about decimals. Use the vocabulary terms *tenths* and *hundredths*.

11 How can you use a 10-by-10 grid to represent decimals?

12 How can you subtract a decimal number from a whole number?

13 How can you add money amounts written in dollar notation?

Word Web

14 Create a word web for the word *point.*

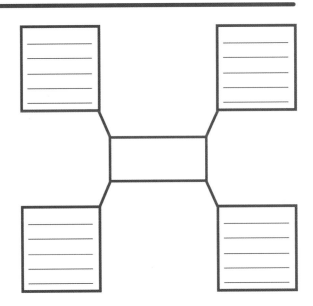

Tree Diagram

15 Create a tree diagram using the words *numbers, whole numbers, fractions,* and *decimals.* Use what you know and what you have learned about fractions and decimals.

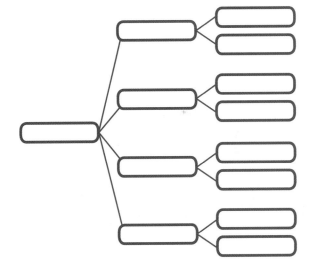

What's in a Word?

DIGITS The word *digits* refers to symbols, such as 0, 1, 2, or 3. The word *digit* comes from a Latin word meaning "finger or toe." So the word *digits* also can be used to refer to a person's fingers and toes. People have often used fingers to help them count, which may explain why we have exactly 10 digits in our number system.

GAME

Ordering Numbers

Game Purpose
To practice using place value to compare and order numbers

Materials
• Activity Master 69: *Number Cards*

Ordering Numbers

How to Play the Game

1 This is a game for 4, 5, or 6 players. Your group will need 3 copies of Activity Master 69. Cut out all the cards.

2 Mix up all the cards. Place them face down in a pile.

3 One player picks 7 cards and places them face up in the middle of the group.
  • Each player uses the number on each card once to create a 7-digit number. Secretly record your number.
  • Everyone shows their numbers. Work as a group to put the numbers in order from least to greatest.

4 This is how you earn points:
  • 2 points if no one else made up the number
  • 1 point for the smallest number (even if someone else has it)
  • 1 point for the largest number (even if someone else has it)

Example: The digits are 9, 7, 1, 6, 4, 2, 3.

Carlene	Lamont	Reese	Tammi
1,234,679	6,971,324	9,764,321	7,964,321

No one else has it, and it's the smallest number: 3 points.

No one else has it: 2 points.

No one else has it, and it's the largest number: 3 points.

No one else has it: 2 points.

5 Mix the cards and play again. First player to 10 points wins!

Guess My Number

Game Purpose
To practice zooming in between numbers on the number line and to gain experience comparing decimals

How to Play the Game

1 Play this game with a group. Decide who will go first. That player will be the Number Master.

2 The Number Master thinks of a secret number with two digits to the right of the decimal point. The goal is to guess the secret number.

• Draw a long line. Label the endpoints with the whole numbers on either side of the secret number.

• Tell everyone that the secret number is between the two whole numbers.

3 Players ask *yes*-or-*no* questions to zoom in on the secret number on the number line.

4 When the answer is *no,* the Number Master crosses out the section of the number line that does not contain the secret number.

Example: The secret number is 3.67. Jorge asks "Is the number less than 3.5?" The answer is *no.*

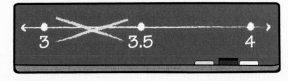

5 Play until someone guesses the secret number. Then choose a different Number Master, and play again. Take turns so that everyone has a chance to be the Number Master.

CHALLENGE

Ayesha and her friends created decimal patterns. Then they made up questions about the patterns to challenge each other.

Student	Pattern
Ayesha	0.14, 0.28, 0.42, 0.56
Luke	5.1, 4.8, 4.5, 4.2
Cameron	0.3, 2, 3.7, 5.4
Tanya	4, 3.64, 3.28, 2.92
Erin	2.5, 4.09, 5.68, 7.27
Seth	12, 10.92, 9.84, 8.76

Use the patterns above to answer the questions.

1 Which patterns increase?

2 Which patterns decrease?

3 Find the next number in each student's pattern.

4 Find the rule for each student's pattern.

5 Find the eighth number in each student's pattern.

6 Write the first number of each pattern in order from smallest to largest.

7 Write the eighth number for each pattern in order from smallest to largest.

Now make up your own decimal pattern.

8 What are the first four terms in your pattern?

9 Does your pattern increase or decrease?

10 Explain the rule you used to create the pattern.

9 Measurement

Dear Student,

This chapter focuses on measurement. You already know quite a bit about measurement. We can measure how long something takes, how hot something is, or how tall we are. What other types of measurement can you think of?

Why is measurement even important? For one thing, it would be hard to tell someone exactly how tall you are without being right next to them and showing them, unless they had something else, like inches and feet, to compare your height to.

You will study various ways to measure length, weight, and volume. For instance, you will see the relations among inches, centimeters, feet, yards, and miles.

As always, we hope you enjoy this unit of measurement!

Mathematically yours,
The authors of *Think Math!*

Ready for Summer!

What is your favorite season: fall, winter, spring, or summer? For many people, summer is the best time of the year. Many families plan summer activities from taking trips to jumping into a backyard pool.

FACT·ACTIVITY 1

1. Noshi's trip will begin on the first day of summer. On June 7th, he begins counting the days until his trip. How many more days until Noshi's trip? How many weeks?

2. Noshi's plane departs at 2:30 P.M. He arrives at the airport at 12:45 P.M. How many minutes until the plane takes off?

3. If the flight is 160 minutes long, how many hours and minutes is the flight?

4. Noshi's return flight from vacation arrives on June 30th at 2:30 P.M. How many days and hours have passed since his plane took off on June 21st?

JUNE

sunday	monday	tuesday	wednesday	thursday	friday	saturday
1	2	3	4	5	6	7
8	9	10	11	12	13	14
15	16	17	18	19	20	21 Summer Begins!
22	23	24	25	26	27	28
29	30					

How do you keep cool in hot weather? There are simple things many families do at home. Some set up sprinklers or use hoses and sheets of plastic to make homemade water slides. Some families set up shallow pools to keep cool.

A family looks at the following two plastic inflatable pools.

Family Swimming Pools			
Name	**Length**	**Width**	**Height**
Blue Lagoon	10 feet	6 feet	1 foot, 10 inches
Clear Blue	5 feet	5 feet	$1\frac{1}{2}$ feet

❶ Katia is 4 feet tall. How many inches taller is she than the top of the Clear Blue pool?

❷ The Blue Lagoon pool is filled up to 6 inches below its height. What will be the height in inches of the water in the pool?

❸ Erik's family wants to enclose the Blue Lagoon pool with fencing. If they have 360 inches of fencing, do they have enough to enclose the pool? Explain why or why not.

CHAPTER PROJECT

Some kids sell lemonade on hot summer days. Plan a lemonade stand. Find a recipe that uses lemons. List the ingredients. How many servings does the recipe make? Suppose you are going to make 5 times the number of servings. Determine how much of each ingredient you will need and list the amounts.

- Weigh one lemon. How many ounces does one lemon weigh? How many total ounces and pounds of lemons will you need?

- How much water does your recipe require? Express the total amount of water you will need in cups, pints, and quarts.

- Fix a price and make a price chart for the cost of 1 to 10 cups of your lemonade.

ALMANAC Fact

Even though Florida is surrounded by the ocean, there are more than 1,000,000 swimming pools in the state.

REVIEW MODEL
Adding Different Units

How can you add dimes $\textcircled{D}$ and nickels $\textcircled{N}$?
How can you add feet and inches?

To add amounts written in different units, change both amounts to the same unit.

Add: 4 nickels + 3 dimes

One Way

Write the amounts in dimes.

4 nickels = 2 dimes
2 dimes + 3 dimes = 5 dimes

Another Way

Write the amounts in nickels.

3 dimes = 6 nickels
4 nickels + 6 nickels = 10 nickels

Another Way

Write the amounts in pennies.

4 nickels = 20 pennies
3 dimes = 30 pennies
20 pennies + 30 pennies = 50 pennies

Add: 5 feet + 6 inches

One Way

Write the amounts in feet.

6 inches = $\frac{1}{2}$ foot

5 feet + $\frac{1}{2}$ foot = $5\frac{1}{2}$ feet

Another Way

Write the amounts in inches.

1 foot = 12 inches
5 feet = 5 × 12 inches = 60 inches
60 inches + 6 inches = 66 inches

✓ Check for Understanding

Add.

1 6 nickels + 3 dimes

2 8 nickels + 4 dimes

3 3 feet + 6 inches

4 4 feet + 3 inches

REVIEW MODEL
Reading an Inch Ruler

An inch ruler can be marked in inches, $\frac{1}{2}$ inches, $\frac{1}{4}$ inches, and $\frac{1}{8}$ inches. Some are marked in $\frac{1}{16}$ inches as well. Follow these steps to read a measurement on an inch ruler.

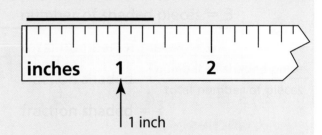

Step 1 Line up the left end of the object you are measuring with zero on the ruler. Count inches, starting at zero. Stop counting at the last inch mark before the end of the line.

1 inch

Step 2 Begin at the last inch mark. Identify the ruler mark closest to the right end of the object you are measuring.

The line is $1\frac{3}{8}$ inches long.

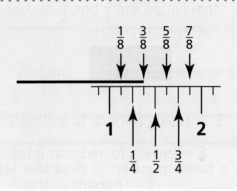

✔Check for Understanding

Find the length of the line.

1

2

3

EXPLORE
Measuring with a Broken Ruler

The fifth grade borrowed all of our rulers except a broken one. Use the broken ruler to check the lengths of these lines.

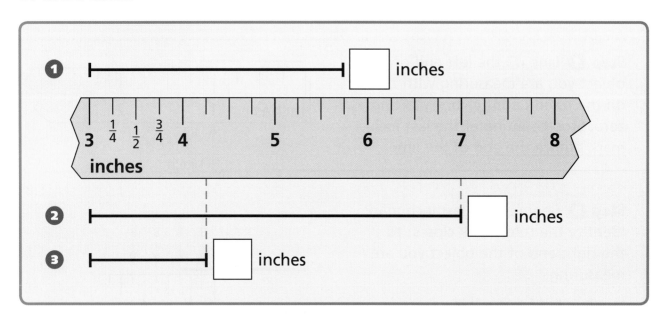

1 ☐ inches

3   $\frac{1}{4}$ $\frac{1}{2}$ $\frac{3}{4}$ 4   5   6   7   8
inches

2 ☐ inches

3 ☐ inches

Now use a broken ruler to find the lengths of these lines.

4 ⊢————————————⊣

5 ⊢————————————————⊣

6 ⊢————————————⊣

7 ⊢——————————————————⊣

8 ⊢————————⊣

REVIEW MODEL
Converting Inches and Feet

You can convert between measurements in inches and measurements in feet.
Remember: **1 foot = 12 inches.**

Convert 4 feet to inches.

Step 1 Think: each 1 foot in the measurement is equal to 12 inches.

1 foot	1 foot	1 foot	1 foot
12 inches	12 inches	12 inches	12 inches

This is four groups of 12.
I'll **multiply** 4 by 12.

Step 2 Multiply. 4 × 12 = 48
So, 4 feet = 48 inches.

Convert 72 inches to feet.

Step 1 Think: a group of 12 inches in the measurement is a foot.

12 inches	12 inches	12 inches	12 inches	12 inches	12 inches
1 foot	1 foot	1 foot	1 foot	1 foot	1 foot

How many groups of 12 inches are in 72 inches?
I'll **divide** 72 by 12.

Step 2 Divide. 72 ÷ 12 = 6
So, 72 inches = 6 feet.

✓ Check for Understanding

Convert.

1 7 feet to inches

2 36 inches to feet

3 5 feet to inches

4 96 inches to feet

EXPLORE
Measuring Length with Cuisenaire® Rods

1 Use the fact that the white rod is 1 centimeter long to find the width of your hand, not including your thumb.

2 How wide is your hand with your thumb?

3 How long is your hand from wrist to fingertip?

4 How long is your shortest finger?

---

5 Using one hand as a ruler, estimate the distance from your elbow to your wrist on your opposite arm.

6 Using your hand as a ruler, estimate the length of your foot.

---

7 Using your hand as a ruler, estimate the width of the back of your chair.

8 Use a centimeter ruler to measure the back of your chair more precisely.

REVIEW MODEL
Reading a Centimeter Ruler

A centimeter ruler is marked in centimeters and millimeters. Follow these steps to read a measurement on a centimeter ruler. Remember: **1 centimeter = 10 millimeters**.

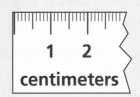

Step ❶ Line up the left end of the object you are measuring with zero on the ruler. Count centimeters, starting at zero. Stop counting at the last centimeter mark before the end of the line.

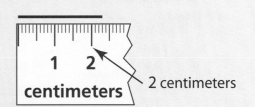

2 centimeters

Step ❷ Begin at the last centimeter mark. Each small mark on the ruler represents 1 millimeter (mm). Identify the millimeter mark at the right end of the object you are measuring.

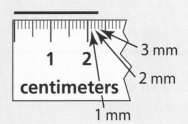

3 mm
2 mm
1 mm

Step ❸ Write the measurement as a decimal number. Write the number of centimeters to the left of the decimal point and the number of millimeters to the right.

The line is **2.3** centimeters long.

✓Check for Understanding

Find the length of the line.

❶

❷

❸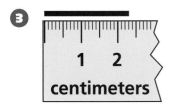

❹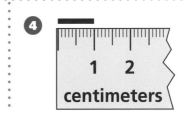

EXPLORE
What is a Cup?

Use a drinking cup or a cup from home to answer these questions.

1 Can your own cup hold more or less than a measuring cup? How do you know?

2 Now pick up a handful of rice, beans, or whatever your teacher supplies. Estimate how many of your handfuls make a standard cup and then measure to check your estimate.

3 Now use a standard measuring cup to find out how much your cup will hold.

EXPLORE
Weight

You can measure weight in ounces, pounds, or tons.

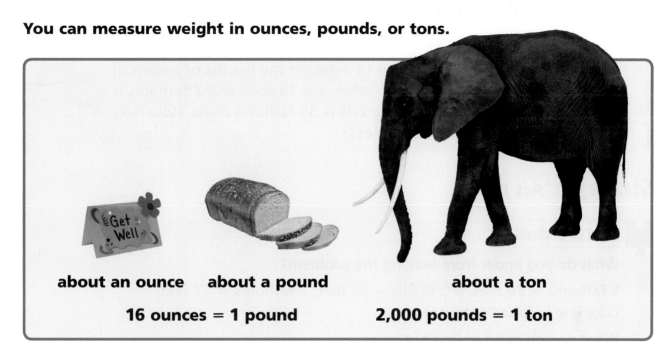

about an ounce   **about a pound**

16 ounces = 1 pound

about a ton

2,000 pounds = 1 ton

1 How many ounces are in a ton?

2 Think about the following questions carefully.

A Which is heavier, 1 cup of feathers or 1 cup of marbles?

B Which is heavier, 1 pound of feathers or 1 pound of marbles?

3 Compare the weights of different objects and decide which
is heavier. Things you might want to compare include:

- a pint of corn flakes and a pint of corn kernels

- a cup of oil and a cup of water

- a quart of sand and a quart of rice

- a cup of dried pasta and a cup of cooked pasta

How do you know which item is heavier?

REVIEW MODEL
Problem Solving Strategy
Look for a Pattern

A *fathom* is a unit of length used to measure the depths of bodies of water. Five fathoms is 30 feet, 6 fathoms is 36 feet, and 7 fathoms is 42 feet. At its deepest point, Lake Erie is 35 fathoms deep. How deep is the deepest point in Lake Erie in feet?

Strategy: Act It Out

Read to Understand

What do you know from reading the problem?

5 fathoms = 30 feet, 6 fathoms = 36 feet, 7 fathoms = 42 feet; Lake Erie is 35 fathoms deep.

What do you need to find out?

Lake Erie's depth in feet

Plan

How can you solve this problem?

You can *look for a pattern* in the given depths and use it to find the length of a fathom.

Solve

What is the pattern in the given depths?

From the given information, I can see that each additional fathom is 6 feet more than the last. So, 1 fathom = 6 feet. I can find the depth of Lake Erie by multiplying its depth in fathoms by 6 feet: $35 \times 6 = 210$. So, Lake Erie is 210 feet deep at its deepest point.

5 fathoms = 30 feet
6 fathoms = 36 feet
7 fathoms = 42 feet

Check

Look back at the problem. Did you answer the questions that were asked? Does the answer make sense?

Yes. To check if the answer makes sense, I could make a table showing fathom depths up to 35 fathoms.

Problem Solving Practice

Use the strategy _look for a pattern_ to solve.

1 A _furlong_ is a unit of measure. 1 mile = 8 furlongs, 2 miles = 16 furlongs, and 3 miles = 24 furlongs. It is 72 furlongs from South City to Meadville. How many miles is it between the towns?

2 Greg scored 72 on his first quiz, 76 on his second quiz, and 80 on his third quiz. His scores continued to increase in the same pattern. On which quiz did he score 100?

Problem Solving Strategies

- ✔ Act It Out
- ✔ Draw a Picture
- ✔ Guess and Check
- ✔ **Look for a Pattern**
- ✔ Make a Graph
- ✔ Make a Model
- ✔ Make an Organized List
- ✔ Make a Table
- ✔ Solve a Simpler Problem
- ✔ Use Logical Reasoning
- ✔ Work Backward
- ✔ Write an Equation

Mixed Strategy Practice

Use any strategy to solve. Explain.

3 Sheila had a rectangular photo with a perimeter of 30 inches. The photo was 3 inches longer than it was wide. What was the area of the photo?

4 Penny bought 2 sweaters each priced at $29 and 3 shirts each priced at $9. She paid for her purchase with a $100 bill. How much change did she receive?

5 Pedro's age is a multiple of 14. His older brother was 20 when their younger cousin was born. His brother is now 50. How old is Pedro?

6 Three apples cost $1.29. Julia bought 5 apples. How much did they cost?

7 Sue is in front of Todd. Becky is behind Andy but ahead of Sue. From front to back, what is the order in which the four are standing?

8 Teresa started to read a 284-page book. For the first 5 days, she read 28 pages each day. How many pages did Teresa have left to read?

9 What number is missing from the table?

Number of fathoms	1	2	3	4
Number of feet	6	12	■	24

10 Ted listened to 86 songs in 4 hours. About how long would it take him to listen to 130 songs?

**Choose the best vocabulary term from Word List A
for each sentence.**

Word List A

centimeter
cup
degree
foot
gallon
inch
length
liter
milliliter
pint
pound
quart
ton
unit
weight
yard

1 A(n) __?__ is the unit used for measuring temperature.

2 You can measure __?__ in ounces, pounds, or tons.

3 The measurement of an object from end to end is its __?__.

4 The __?__ is a customary unit for measuring capacity equal to
16 cups.

5 One __?__ is exactly 3 feet long.

6 A fish tank holding 240 gallons of water weighs
about 1 __?__.

7 One __?__ in the metric system is about the same as 1 quart
in the customary system.

8 One hundredth of a meter is 1 __?__.

9 A(n) __?__ is one twelfth of a foot.

10 Four cups are the same as 1 __?__.

**Complete each analogy. Use the best term from
Word List B.**

Word List B

gallon
inch
liter
pound
quart
yard

11 Foot is to length as __?__ is to weight.

12 Cup is to pint as half-gallon is to __?__.

Talk Math

**Discuss with a partner what you have learned about
measurement. Use the vocabulary terms *cup*, *gallon*,
pint, and *quart*.**

13 How can you find the number of cups in a gallon?

14 Suppose you know the number of gallons you have.
How can you find how many cups you have?

Analysis Chart

15 Create an analysis chart for the terms *inch, foot, yard,* and *centimeter.* Use what you know and what you have learned about measures of length.

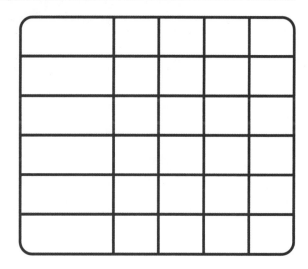

Word Web

16 Create a word web using the term *pound.*

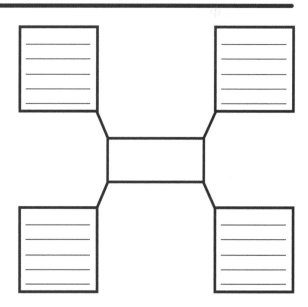

YARD A *yard* is not always a unit of measurement. Someone's house might have a front *yard*. This type of *yard* comes from the Old English word *geard,* which means "an enclosed space."

In mathematics, the word *yard* comes from the Old English word *gierd,* which means "twig." Originally, a *yard* measured about 5 meters. Later, the *yard* became a standard length of 3 feet. This is the measure we use today.

GAME

Target Temperatures

Game Purpose
To practice adding and subtracting temperatures

Materials
- Activity Master 82: The Target Temperatures Game
- Activity Master 83: Target Temperature
- 1 small game piece, such as centimeter cube
- 2 number cubes (labeled 1–6)

How To Play The Game

1 This game is for 2 players.
- Mix up the Target Temperature cards. Place them face down in a pile.
- Put the game piece at 60°F on the game board.

2 Turn the top card face up. This is the target temperature. Your goal is to land on this temperature.

3 Partners take turns.
- Roll the two number cubes.
- Use either the sum or difference of the numbers you rolled. Move the game piece that many degrees in either direction—warmer or colder.

4 If you land on the target temperature, keep the card. Turn the next card of the deck face up. This is the new target temperature. Keep playing.

5 The game ends when all of the Target Temperature cards have been collected.

6 The player with the most cards at the end of the game wins.

GAME

Build-a-Foot

Game Purpose
To practice using Cuisenaire® Rods to find lengths in centimeters
To relate centimeters to inches

Materials
- Activity Master 86: Spinner
- Inch ruler
- Paper clip and pencil
- Cuisenaire® Rods

Build-a-Foot

How To Play The Game

1 Play this game with a partner. Each player will build a train of Cuisenaire® Rods. The goal is to estimate when the length of your train is close to 1 foot. If you can estimate the length to within 1 centimeter, you win.

2 First, make a spinner using Activity Master 86: Spinner. Put the point of a pencil through one end of the paper clip. Put the tip of the pencil on the center of the spinner. Then you can spin the paper clip around the pencil.

3 Take turns spinning the spinner. Collect the Cuisenaire® Rod shown by your spin.

4 Make a train of rods by placing them end-to-end.

5 When you think your train is 1 foot long, use the ruler to check.
- If your train is more than 1 centimeter shorter or longer than a foot, you must remove the rod added to the train. If your train is longer than a foot, remove pieces until it is less than a foot long.
- If your train is within 1 centimeter of a foot, you win!

CHALLENGE

Have you ever wondered how to measure distances around a curve?

All you need is a piece of string that is about **12** inches long and a ruler. Use these materials to measure the distance of the five trips on this map of Washington, D.C.

The map shows a highway called the Beltway that circles Washington, D.C. On the map, the Beltway is Interstate **495**.

For each trip, place the string on the map where you get on the Beltway. Follow the road with the string to where you get off. Then use the scale on the map to estimate the distance you would travel on the Beltway in miles.

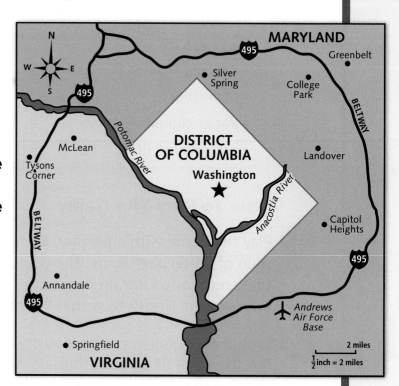

1 From McLean, VA, to Annandale, VA

2 From Greenbelt, MD, to Capitol Heights, MD

3 South from College Park, MD, to Springfield, VA

4 South from Landover, MD, to Tysons Corner, VA

5 North from Andrews Air Force Base, MD, to Silver Spring, MD

10 Data and Probability

Dear Student,

If you toss a coin, how likely is it that the coin will come up heads? If you toss a coin 10 times in a row, about how many times would you expect to get heads? Could you get 10 heads in a row? Would it surprise you if that happened?

These are all questions about probability: how likely it is that some particular thing will happen.

Imagine a machine that prints out cards with figures on them. There are three possible figures: a parallelogram, a trapezoid, and a triangle. The figures can be either blue or green, and either striped or solid-colored. You can set each of the levers separately to pick the color, shape, and pattern that the machine will print on a card. In this picture, the machine has been set to print a solid blue trapezoid.

How many different combinations of color, shape, and pattern do you think the machine can make? How many of those combinations would be blue figures?

If you set the switches without looking, how likely is it that the machine will print a blue figure? You'll be talking about questions like this as you learn about probability.

Mathematically yours,
The authors of *Think Math!*

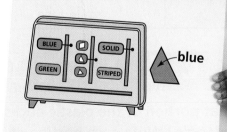

159

You Quack Me Up!

Whether it is a state fair, a county fair, or a school fair, there is something for everyone to smile about at a fair.

There is a children's duck pond game at Center Elementary School Fair. Twelve plastic ducks are in the pond and each duck has a star, circle, or triangle hidden on its bottom. You pick a duck at random from the pond. You will win a pencil top eraser prize depending on which symbol is on the bottom of the duck you pick. The table shows how many ducks have each symbol, and which pencil top eraser you will receive.

Duck Pond Game		
Symbol	**Pencil Top Eraser**	**Number of Ducks**
★	dinosaur	2
●	train	4
▲	smile face	6

FACT·ACTIVITY 1:

❶ What portion of the plastic ducks have a star? a circle? a triangle? Write each portion as a fraction.

❷ If you pick a plastic duck at random, which pencil top eraser are you most likely to receive?

❸ How many ducks with stars would there have to be to make the likelihood of receiving a dinosaur pencil top eraser $\frac{1}{12}$?

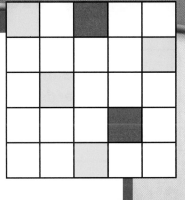

Another game at the school fair has a grid of squares with different colors. You toss a bean bag onto the grid. You then receive a pencil with a special message depending on the color of the square your bag lands on.

Bean Bag Toss Game	
Color	**Message**
White	Have a great day!
Yellow	You are so cool!
Red	Kids rule!

FACT·ACTIVITY 2

Use the chart and grid to answer the questions.

1 If your bag is equally likely to land on each square, what fraction of the game board wins the pencils that say, *Have a great day!; You are so cool!; Kids rule!*?

Olivia played the game 10 times and landed on: white, white, yellow, white, yellow, white, white, white, red, white.

2 Draw a bar graph to show the results of Olivia's 10 throws.

3 Based on Olivia's results, what fraction of the pencils she won say, *Have a great day! or Kids rule!*?

CHAPTER PROJECT

Sometimes spinners are used in games of chance. Design your own *Spin the Wheel* game. Draw a circle on cardboard. Divide the circle into 6 or 12 equal sections. Fill the sections using 3 different colors. Cut out the circle. Put the tip of a pencil through the center of the circle's top side. Place a paper clip around the pencil tip. Flick the paper clip to make it spin. Describe the rules of your game. Which color is the spinner most likely to land on? least likely?

- Play the game 20 times and collect the data. Show the data in a table and a bar graph.

- Using your table, determine the probability of each outcome as a fraction. Make a prediction of the next spin.

ALMANAC Fact

The first Texas State Fair was held in Fair Park, Dallas in 1886. Today, the 277-acre Fair Park is an education, entertainment, and recreation center where you can find museums, a music hall, and the famous Cotton Bowl Stadium.

EXPLORE
How Likely is It?

> Becky and Sammi played "Fish" with the deck of attribute cards. Becky said the game wasn't fair because some kinds of cards came up more often than others. You decide to explore this idea.

1 If you draw one card from your deck of attribute cards, what might it be? List all possibilities.

2 If you draw one card from your deck, is it *certain*, *likely*, *unlikely*, or *impossible* that the card will have a figure that is:

- either striped or solid?

- either a parallelogram or a triangle?

- a trapezoid?

- yellow?

- a blue trapezoid?

- green or striped or both?

Be prepared to explain and discuss why you chose your answer.

3 Think of some other possibilities that are *certain*, *likely*, *unlikely*, or *impossible* if you draw one attribute card.

REVIEW MODEL
Writing Probabilities

What is the probability of choosing a shaded card?

A A A B B B C C

You can use fractions to write probabilities.

Step ❶	**Step ❷**	**Step ❸**
Count to find the number of shaded cards. 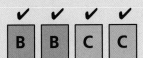 ✔ ✔ ✔ ✔ B B C C There are 4 shaded cards.	Count to find the total number of cards. There are 8 cards altogether.	Write the probability. probability = $\frac{\text{shaded cards}}{\text{total cards}}$ probability = $\frac{4}{8}$ or $\frac{1}{2}$

What is the probability of choosing "B"?

Step ❶	**Step ❷**	**Step ❸**
Count to find the number of "B" cards. 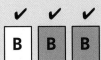 ✔ ✔ ✔ B B B There are 3 "B" cards.	Count to find the total number of cards. There are 8 cards altogether.	Write the probability. probability = $\frac{\text{"B" cards}}{\text{total cards}}$ probability = $\frac{3}{8}$

✔ Check for Understanding

❶ What is the probability of choosing a striped card?

X X X Y Y Y

❷ What is the probability of choosing a "Y"?

❸ What is the probability of choosing an unshaded, unstriped "X"?

EXPLORE
How Likely is Drawing a Trapezoid?

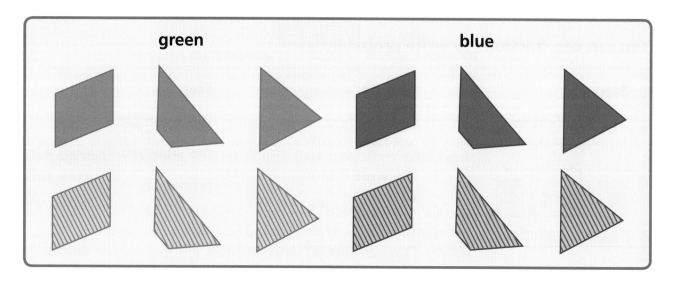

green   blue

Imagine that you:

- **draw one attribute card randomly from the deck**
- **write down what is on the card**
- **return the card to the deck**
- **shuffle the deck**

1 If you repeat these steps 30 times, about how many times do you think you will pick a card with a trapezoid on it?

2 About what fraction of the cards you drew do you predict will have trapezoids?

3 Write at least 3 fractions equivalent to the one you wrote for Problem 2.

REVIEW MODEL
Finding Equivalent Fractions Using Patterns

You can use patterns to write a fraction that is equivalent to another fraction. Look for a relationship between the top and bottom numbers in the first fraction. The relationship should involve multiplication or division. Use the same relationship to write an equivalent fraction.

Find a fraction equivalent to $\frac{2}{6}$.

Step ❶

How are the top and bottom numbers related?

$\frac{2}{6}$ The bottom number is **3** times the top number.

$6 = 3 \times 2$

Step ❷

Use the same relationship to write an equivalent fraction.

One Way

$\frac{1}{3}$ The top number is 1. The bottom number is **3** $\times$ 1.

Another Way

$\frac{5}{15}$ The top number is 5. The bottom number is **3** $\times$ 5.

Find a fraction equivalent to $\frac{8}{10}$.

Step ❶

How are the top and bottom numbers related?

$\frac{8}{10}$ Multiply (or divide) both top and bottom by the same number.

$\frac{8 \div 2}{10 \div 2} = \frac{4}{5}$

Step ❷

Use the new fraction to write an equivalent fraction.

One Way

$\frac{4 \times 3}{5 \times 3} = \frac{12}{15}$

Another Way

$\frac{4 \times 7}{5 \times 7} = \frac{28}{35}$

✔Check for Understanding

❶ Find two fractions equivalent to $\frac{2}{8}$.

❷ Find two fractions equivalent to $\frac{6}{10}$.

EXPLORE
9-Block Experiment

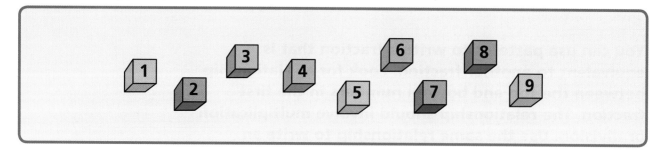

1 If you put these blocks into a bag and drew one without looking, what is the probability that the number on your block would be:

- even?

- a multiple of 3?

- a square number?

- at least 5?

2 If you draw a block as in Problem 1 and do this 27 times, putting the block back each time, about how many blocks would you expect to draw whose number is:

- even?

- a multiple of 3?

- a square number?

- at least 5?

3 Think of at least 2 more predictions you can make about the experiment described in Problem 2.

REVIEW MODEL
Making a Bar Graph

Making a bar graph is like building towers out of blocks. You can compare sets of data by comparing the heights of the towers.

At the right are the results of the Coyotes' first 8 soccer games (W = win, L = loss, T = tie). Draw a bar graph of the results.

RESULTS OF COYOTES' GAMES
W   W   L   T   T   W   T   W

Step ❶

Draw and label a grid. Let the horizontal axis represent the type of game result. Let the vertical axis represent the number of games for each type of data.

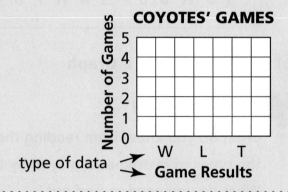

type of data

Step ❷

Graph the data. Start at the bottoms of columns. Shade one square for each win, one square for each loss, and one square for each tie.

The completed graph allows you to compare numbers of wins, losses, and ties visually as well as numerically.

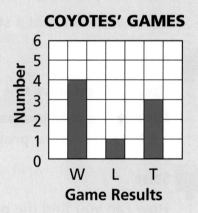

✔Check for Understanding

Below are the ways 15 students get to school (W = walk, C = car, B = bus, S = subway). Draw a bar graph of these means of transportation.

SCHOOL TRANSPORTATION
S   C   B   W   B   C   B   C
S   S   W   B   S   C   B

REVIEW MODEL
Problem Solving Strategy
Make a Graph

Listed below are the types of instrument played by the members of the school band (B = brass, P = percussion, S = string, W = woodwind). One student was absent from rehearsal yesterday. What is the probability that the student plays a brass instrument?

S B W B B P S B W P B W W B S S B S W S B W W P

Strategy: Make a Graph

 Read to Understand

What do you know from reading the problem?

the types of instruments played by the band members

What do you need to find out?

the probability that a student plays a brass instrument

Plan

How can you solve this problem?

Display the data in a bar graph. Then count squares to find the probability.

 Solve

How can you find the probability?

First, make and label a grid. For each item of data, shade a square in the correct column. Eight of the 24 shaded squares represent brass instruments. The probability is $\frac{8}{24}$ or $\frac{1}{3}$.

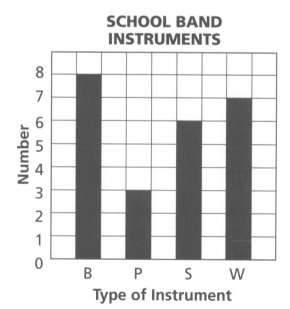

SCHOOL BAND INSTRUMENTS

Check

Look back at the problem. Did you answer the question that was asked? Does the answer make sense?

Problem Solving Practice

Use the strategy _make a graph_ to solve.

1 Ashton tossed a number cube 18 times. She tossed three 1s, two 2s, four 3s, five 4s, zero 5s, and four 6s. Show how she can display the data to allow easy analysis of her results.

2 Look at the graph you made in Problem 1. Which number did Ashton toss the expected number of times? How does the graph show this?

Problem Solving Strategies

✔ Act it Out
✔ Draw a Picture
✔ Guess and Check
✔ Look for a Pattern
✔ **Make a Graph**
✔ Make a Model
✔ Make an Organized List
✔ Make a Table
✔ Solve a Simpler Problem
✔ Use Logical Reasoning
✔ Work Backward
✔ Write an Equation

Mixed Strategy Practice

Use any strategy to solve.

3 Jake scored 100 points total on three math quizzes. He scored 29 and 42 on the first two quizzes. What did he score on the third quiz?

4 A square has an area of 100 square inches. What is the perimeter of the square?

5 Baseball cards sell for $12 each. Football cards sell for $9 each. Mason bought 3 baseball cards and 5 football cards. He paid for his purchase with a $100 bill. How much change did he receive?

6 Movie tickets cost $8. The movie theater has 18 rows of seats with 14 seats in each row. At the last show there were 96 empty seats. How much was spent on the purchase of tickets for that show?

7 Eggs sell for $1.45 per dozen. Becky bought 72 eggs. How much did the eggs cost?

8 Mrs. Fritz is 3 times as old as her son Marco. Her daughter Hallie, who is 7 years old, is half as old as Marco. How old is Mrs. Fritz?

9 Apples sell for $1.56 per pound. Peaches sell for $1.66 per pound. If the price of apples increases 4¢ per week and the price of peaches increases 2¢ per week, what will the price be when both items sell for the same price?

10 Blake scored 28 points in a basketball game. Some of his points came from 2-pointers and the rest came from 3-pointers. He scored twice as many 2-pointers as 3-pointers. How many 3-pointers did he score?

Choose the best vocabulary term from Word List A for each sentence.

❶ A(n) ___?___ is often stated as some number from 0 to 1.

❷ Information can also be called ___?___.

❸ An event with a probability of less than $\frac{1}{2}$ is a(n) ___?___ event.

❹ To find the ___?___ of a set of data, subtract the smallest number from the largest number.

❺ An event with a probability of 1 is a(n) ___?___ event.

❻ An event with a probability of 0 is a(n) ___?___ event.

❼ A measurement of 1 hour has less ___?___ than a measurement of 54 minutes.

❽ A(n) ___?___ is a possible result of an action.

❾ The ___?___ of a set of data is the item that appears more often than any of the other items.

Word List A

attribute
certain
data
impossible
likely
median
mode
outcome
precision
probability
range
unlikely

Complete each analogy. Use the best term from Word List B.

❿ Usually is to ___?___ as always is to certain.

⓫ *B* is to *ABC* as ___?___ is to a set of data.

Word List B

likely
median
probability

🗪 Talk Math

Discuss with a partner what you have just learned about data and probability. Use the vocabulary terms *certain, impossible, likely,* **and** *unlikely.*

⓬ Suppose temperatures increased 2 degrees each day last week. How can you describe temperatures for the next day?

⓭ A coin is flipped 100 times. How can you describe the outcomes?

Word Line

14 Create a word line for the terms *certain, impossible, likely,* and *unlikely.* Arrange the words from 0 to 1.

Words:

Sequence:

_____

Concept Map

15 Create a concept map for *Describe Data.* Use what you have learned about ways to describe a set of data.

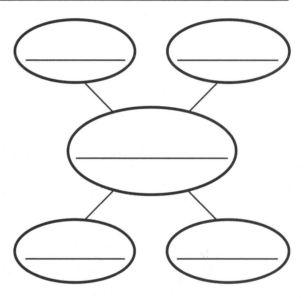

What's in a Word?

DATA Ancient Romans did not have e-mail, so they wrote messages by hand. At the end of a message, they wrote *"datum,"* meaning "given" and the month and day. More than one *datum* is *data.* The Romans used *data* to mean "the time and place stated."

Today, we use the word *data* to mean information collected about people or things. Weights, heights, lengths, dates, and populations are all *data.*

GAME

Attribute Memory

Game Purpose
To practice identifying common attributes

Materials
- Activity Master 90: Machine Cards
- blue and green pencils
- scissors

Attribute Memory

How To Play The Game

1 Play this game with 3 players. On, Activity Master 90, shade the top 6 figures blue. Shade the bottom 6 figures green. Cut out the cards.

2 Mix up the cards, and place all 12 face down in a 4-by-3 array.

3 The first player turns over two cards.
- If the figures on the cards have two attributes in common and one that is different, the player keeps the cards.
- If the figures have no attributes in common, the player puts the cards back face down where they were in the array.

Example:

You could keep this pair.	You could not keep this pair.
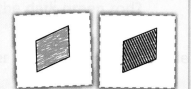	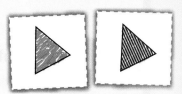
The shape and color are the same, but the shading is different.	**The shape is the same, but the shading and color are different.**

4 Players take turns repeating Step 3 until no more cards can be taken. There could be up to 4 cards left on the table when no more can be taken.

5 The player with the greatest number of cards wins.

GAME

Attribute Card Forecast

Game Purpose
To practice estimating probabilities

Materials
- Set of 12 Attribute Cards
- Activity Masters 92, 93, and 94
  (Event Cards)

How To Play The Game

1 Play this game with 3 or 4 players.
- Mix up the Attribute Cards. Place the pile of Attribute Cards face down on the table.
- Mix up the Event Cards. Pass out the Event Cards equally among the players. Set aside any leftover cards.
- Decide who will go first.

2 Player 1 chooses one Event Card from his or her cards and puts it face up on the table. The other players take turns doing the same, moving clockwise from Player 1.

3 Player 1 turns the top Attribute Card face up.

4 Any player whose Event Card describes the Attribute Card scores 1 point. The description must be correct. It does not have to be complete.

Example: For this round, two Attribute cards are correct. Can you find them?

5 Put the Attribute Card back in the pile, and mix up the cards.

6 Repeat Steps 2–4. This time, the player to the left of Player 1 goes first.

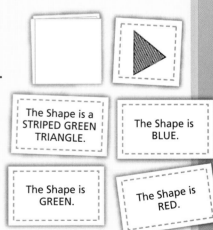

The Shape is a STRIPED GREEN TRIANGLE.

The Shape is BLUE.

The Shape is GREEN.

The Shape is RED.

7 Play the game until all the Event Cards have been used. The player with the greatest number of points is the winner.

CHALLENGE

Play these games with a partner. You'll need two number cubes labeled 1 to 6. Decide who will be Player 1 and Player 2 for each game. Play both games several times. Then use what you know about probability to decide whether each is a fair game. Any game is fair if all players have an equal chance of winning.

Play a Subtraction Game

❶ Take turns tossing both number cubes and subtracting the smaller number from the larger number.

- Player 1 gets 1 point if the difference is an odd number.
- Player 2 gets 1 point if the difference is an even number. Remember, 0 is an even number.

❷ The first player with 10 points wins the game. Play again.

❸ After you have played several times, copy the above table. Complete the table, and use it to help you decide if this a fair game.

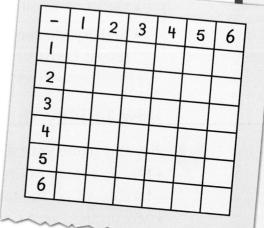

−	1	2	3	4	5	6
1						
2						
3						
4						
5						
6						

Play a Multiplication Game

❶ Take turns tossing both cubes and multiplying the numbers.

- Player 1 gets 1 point if the product is an odd number.
- Player 2 gets 1 point if the product is an even number.

❷ The first player with 10 points wins the game. Play again.

❸ After you have played several times, copy this table. Complete the table, and use it to help you decide if this a fair game.

×	1	2	3	4	5	6
1						
2						
3						
4						
5						
6						

Chapter

11 Three-Dimensional Geometry

Dear Student,

Three-dimensional objects have height, width, and depth. Most such objects, especially those that occur in nature, have complicated shapes (think of trees, people, and clouds). But many things that people make have simple three-dimensional shapes (think of milk cartons, tin cans, the room you're in, and spaghetti). Even some natural objects such as crystals and water drops have simple shapes.

In this chapter, you'll explore many such simple shapes. You'll make some of them by folding paper.

Some three-dimensional figures have curved surfaces. If all the surfaces of a figure are flat, we call that figure a *polyhedron*. In this chapter you'll learn why we refer to the surfaces of a polyhedron as "faces," rather than the more familiar word "sides." You'll find the total area of a polyhedron's faces, which tells how much paper you would need to wrap the polyhedron if you were giving it to someone as a gift. And you'll learn how to measure the volume *inside* a polyhedron, which tells the amount of air, water, wood, or metal it could contain.

Now, it's time to start building! Have fun!

Mathematically yours,
The authors of *Think Math!*

Wrapping It Up!

Cardboard was invented in China in the 1600s. About 200 years later the English used cardboard to make cardboard boxes.

FACT·ACTIVITY 1

Luka, Megan, Nate, and Olivia each buy a toy from a toy shop. The toys are packaged in cardboard boxes of various shapes.

Use the toy boxes to answer 1–4.

1 Name the three-dimensional figure represented by each toy box.

2 Describe the faces of Megan's toy box. How many faces are there? Are the faces congruent to each other?

3 Which person's toy box has faces in which all of the angles are congruent? Describe the angles.

4 Which of the nets below is a net for Megan's toy box?

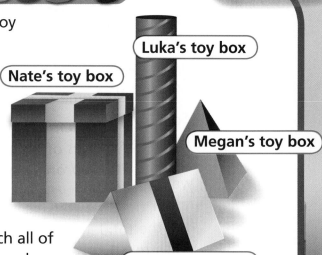

Luka's toy box

Nate's toy box

Megan's toy box

Olivia's toy box

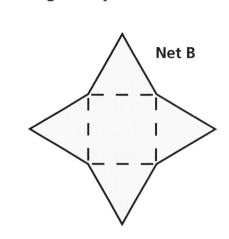

Net A

Net B

People have been wrapping gifts for almost 2,000 years when paper was invented in China. Today, you can buy all sorts of fancy gift wrap.

Max needs to wrap this gift box.

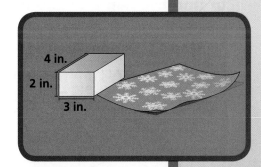

1 Trace the net below on a piece of paper. Label the net with the measurements of each edge using the box drawing at the right.

2 Find the total area of the faces of the box.

3 Suppose Max's gift wrap measures 5 in. × 10 in. Does he have enough to wrap the box? Explain.

4 Max wants to fill the box with candy that originally filled a box that was 6 in. long, 2 in. wide, and 2 in. high. Will the candy fit in the box? Explain.

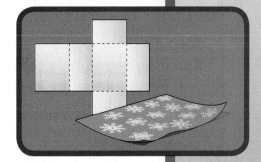

CHAPTER PROJECT

Materials: empty boxes, one-inch cubes, inch ruler

How good are you at estimating volume? Work in groups of 3 or more. Gather a collection of empty boxes shaped like rectangular prisms, such as cereal boxes, shoe boxes, or tissue boxes. Use various sizes.

- Write down the number of one-inch cubes you think will fit in each box. Carefully place as many cubes as you can in each box. Record your results. Compare your estimates to the number of cubes that actually fit in the boxes.

- Then, measure to the nearest inch the length, width, and height of each box and find the volume for each box. Record your results.

- How do you explain the difference between the volume found by placing the cubes in the box and the volume found using the formula?

ALMANAC
Fact

Edwin Binney and C. Harold Smith made their first box of crayons in 1903. There were only 8 colors back then. They now make bigger boxes with as many as 120 colors.

REVIEW MODEL
Recognizing Three-Dimensional Figures

You can use the faces of a three-dimensional figure to find the name of the figure.

Step 1 Decide: Are the faces flat and polygon-shaped?

YES. The faces are flat and polygon-shaped. The figure is a **polyhedron.**

NO. At least one face is curved. The figure is *not* a **polyhedron.**

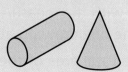

Step 2 If the shape is a polyhedron, decide: Can it be placed on a table so that the top and bottom faces are parallel and congruent?

YES. The figure is a **prism.**

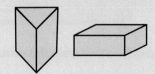

NO. The figure is *not* a **prism.** But if it can sit flat on one face on a table, and if its other faces are triangles that meet at a point, it is a **pyramid.**

Step 3 If at least one face is curved, decide: Does it have a sharp point?

YES. The figure is a **cone.**

NO. The figure is *not* a **cone.** But if it can be placed on a table so that the top and bottom faces are parallel and congruent, it is a **cylinder.**

✔Check for Understanding

Name the figure.

1

2

3

4

EXPLORE
Finding Areas

The faces of Figure B are all rectangles.

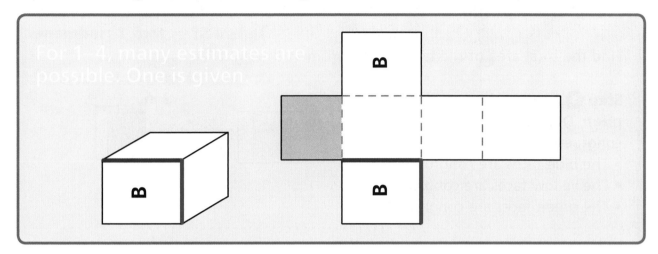

For 1–4, many estimates are possible. One is given.

Use the net of Figure B page to answer these questions.

1 Estimate the length of the green edge of Face B in inches.

2 Estimate the length of the blue edge of Face B in inches.

3 Estimate the area of Face B in square inches.

4 Estimate the perimeter of the net of Figure B.

Use a ruler to measure the edges of Figure B.

5 Using your measurements, find the perimeter of the net of Figure B.

6 Using your measurements, find the area of Face B in square inches.

7 Using your measurements, find the area of the shaded face in square inches.

8 Find the total area of all of the faces of this polyhedron in square inches.

REVIEW MODEL
Finding Areas of Faces

You can use the net of a prism to find the total area of the faces of the prism.

Find the total area of the faces of the prism at the right.

Step 1 Look at the net of the prism. Decide which faces are congruent.
- The blue faces are congruent.
- The yellow faces are congruent.
- The green faces are congruent.

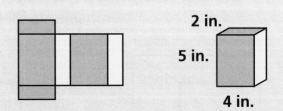

2 in.
5 in.
4 in.

Step 2 Use the prism to find the length and width of each different face.

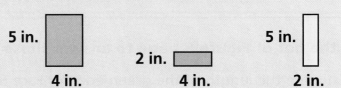

5 in.
4 in.

2 in.
4 in.

5 in.
2 in.

Step 3 Multiply the length by the width to find the area of each face.

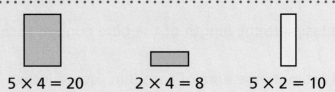

$5 \times 4 = 20$ $2 \times 4 = 8$ $5 \times 2 = 10$

Step 4 Add the areas of the faces to find the total area. Remember to include the areas of the congruent faces.

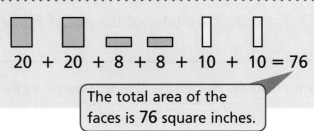

$20 + 20 + 8 + 8 + 10 + 10 = 76$

> The total area of the faces is 76 square inches.

✔Check for Understanding

Find the total area of the faces of the prism.

1

3 in.
8 in.
5 in.

2

5 in.
5 in.
5 in.

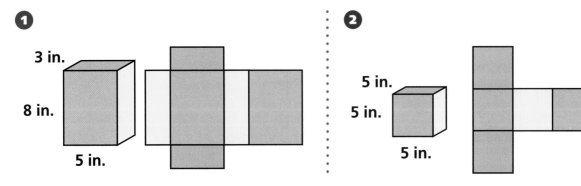

EXPLORE
Exploring Volume

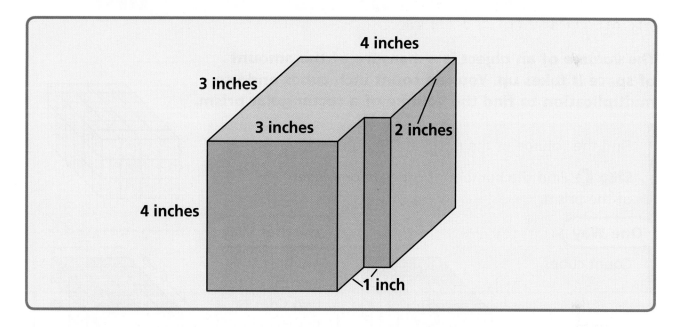

In a minute, you're going to build this three-dimensional figure out of inch cubes.

❶ How many cubes do you think you will need?

Now build the shapes with cubes.

❷ How many cubes did you use?

REVIEW MODEL
Finding the Volume of a Three-Dimensional Figure

The *volume* of an object is a measure of the amount of space it takes up. You can count inch cubes and use multiplication to find the volume of a rectangular prism.

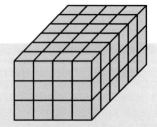

Find the volume of the prism at the right.

Step ❶ Find the number of cubes in **one layer** of the prism.

One Way

Count cubes.

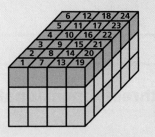

There are 24 cubes in the top layer.

Another Way

Multiply the lengths of the two sides of the layer.

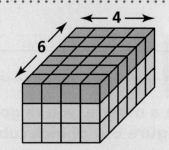

There are 24 cubes in the top layer.

Step ❷ Multiply your answer by the number of layers in the prism.

$$3 \times 24 = 72$$

The volume of the prism is 72 cubic units.

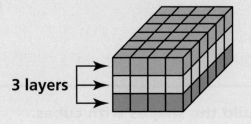

3 layers

✔ Check for Understanding

Find the volume of the rectangular prism.

❶

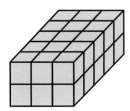

❷

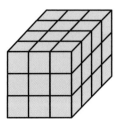

EXPLORE
Prisms with the Same Volume

Shelby built this 3 inch × 2 inch × 6 inch rectangular prism.

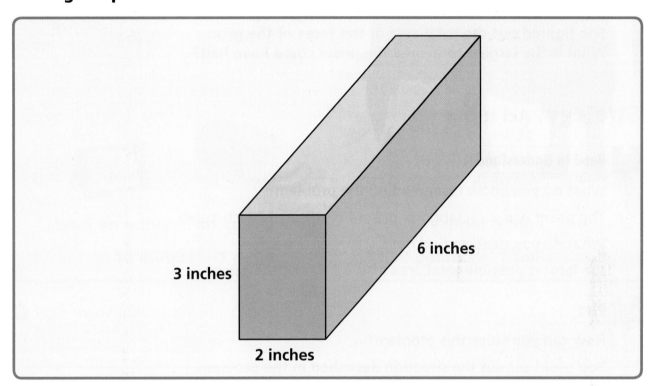

6 inches

3 inches

2 inches

❶ Build and then draw a sketch of a different rectangular prism with the same volume as Shelby's prism. Write an expression like the following to describe your prism.

3 in. × 2 in. × 6 in.

❷ Try to build another rectangular prism with this same volume. Write an expression to describe your prism.

REVIEW MODEL
Problem Solving Strategy
Act It Out

> Gina used **12** inch-cubes to build a rectangular prism.
> She figured out the total area of the faces of the prism.
> What is the largest total area the prism could have had?

Strategy: Act It Out

Read to Understand

What do you know from reading the problem?

The prism was a rectangular prism built from **12** inch-cubes.

What do you need to find out?

the largest possible total area of the faces of the prism

Plan

How can you solve this problem?

You could act out the situation described in the problem.

Solve

How can you act out the problem?

You can build all possible rectangular prisms using **12** inch-cubes. Then you can find the total areas of their faces by counting the faces of the cubes. Each face has an area of **1** square inch.

Four prisms are possible:

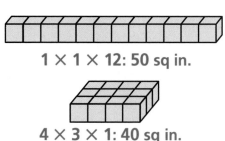

$1 \times 1 \times 12$: 50 sq in.

$3 \times 2 \times 2$: 32 sq in.

$4 \times 3 \times 1$: 40 sq in.

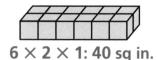

$6 \times 2 \times 1$: 40 sq in.

The largest possible total area is **50** square inches.

Check

Look back at the problem. Did you answer the question that was asked? Does the answer make sense?

Problem Solving Practice

Use the strategy _act it out_ to solve.

1 A man and his wife each weigh 160 pounds. Each of their twin sons weighs 80 pounds. The four must cross a stream in a rowboat that holds only 160 pounds. How can they cross the stream?

2 A rectangular piece of wood measures 3 feet by 6 feet. A carpenter wants to cut the board into three pieces that can be joined together to make a board measuring 2 feet by 9 feet. How can the carpenter do this?

Problem Solving Strategies

✔ **Act It Out**
✔ Draw a Picture
✔ Guess and Check
✔ Look for a Pattern
✔ Make a Graph
✔ Make a Model
✔ Make an Organized List
✔ Make a Table
✔ Solve a Simpler Problem
✔ Use Logical Reasoning
✔ Work Backward
✔ Write an Equation

Mixed Strategy Practice

Use any strategy to solve.

3 The drawing shows that exactly two lines can be drawn from a corner of a 5-sided polygon to other corners. How many lines can be drawn from a corner of a 25-sided polygon to other corners?

4 An empty room is in the shape of a rectangular prism measuring 15 feet by 12 feet by 8 feet. Suppose you painted all four walls, the ceiling, and the floor. How many gallons of paint would you need if each gallon covered an area of 300 square feet?

5 A rectangle with a perimeter of 30 inches is twice as long as it is wide. What is the area of the rectangle?

6 Jon bought twelve 39-cent stamps and paid for them with a $10 bill. How many 4-cent stamps can he buy with the change he received?

7 Christy ran for an hour around a track that was 500 yards long. Her average speed was 8 miles per hour. How far did she run?

8 Lee, Kara, and Jared are shelving books in the library. Lee took half the books. Kara took two-thirds of the books that remained. Jared took the last 6 books. How many books were there to begin with?

Choose the best vocabulary term from Word List A for each sentence.

Word List A

area
edge
face
height
net
polyhedron
prism
pyramid
side
vertex
volume
width

❶ A polygon that is one side of a polyhedron is called a(n) ___?___.

❷ A polyhedron with a polygon base and other faces that are triangles is a(n) ___?___.

❸ The place where three or more edges of a polyhedron intersect is called a(n) ___?___.

❹ A three-dimensional figure with polygonal faces is called a(n) ___?___.

❺ A polyhedron with two congruent polygonal bases and other faces that are rectangles is a(n) ___?___.

❻ A line segment that forms the boundary of a face of a polyhedron is called a(n) ___?___.

❼ A(n) ___?___ is a two-dimensional pattern of a three-dimensional figure.

Complete each analogy using the best term from Word List B.

Word List B

cube
length
total area
vertex

❽ Square is to area as ___?___ is to volume.

❾ ___?___ is to vertices as polyhedron is to polyhedra.

⬭ Talk Math

Discuss with a partner what you have learned about polyhedra. Use the vocabulary terms *face, net,* and *three-dimensional figure.*

❿ How can you recognize a polyhedron?

⓫ How are prisms and pyramids similar? How are they different?

⓬ How can you find the surface area of a polyhedron?

Venn Diagram

13 Create a Venn diagram for the words *area, cubic, face, length, height, nets, polyhedron, total area, volume,* and *width.*

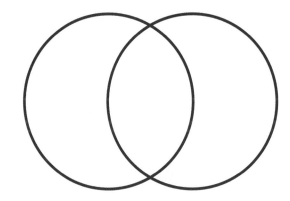

Tree Diagram

14 Create a tree diagram using the word *polyhedra.* Use what you know and what you have learned about three-dimensional figures.

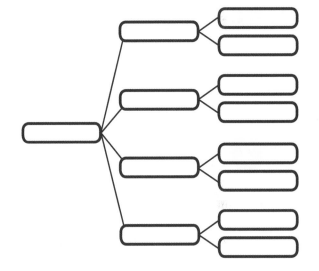

FACE *Face* usually means the front of something. The front of your head from your chin to your forehead is your *face.* Other fronts are the *face* of a building, the *face* of a clock, and the *face* of the moon. *Face* is also an action, such as "*face* the board," which means "turn toward the board." In math, *face* has a meaning similar to "front." A *face* is any of the plane surfaces of a polyhedron.

GAME

Figure Sit Down

Game Purpose
To practice identifying attributes of three-dimensional figures

Materials
- Figure Zoo figures from **Lesson 11.1**
- Index cards

Figure Sit Down

It has 6 faces.

It has more than 5 vertices.

It has fewer than 8 right angles.

Some faces are triangles.

How To Play The Game

1 This is a game for a group of **6** to **10** players. Together, make a set of Attribute Cards. Write a different attribute of a three-dimensional figure on an index card. Write as many as you can think of. Try not to write attributes that belong to all prisms or all pyramids. Here are some suggestions:

2 Decide who will be the Zookeeper. The Zookeeper mixes up all the Attribute Cards and puts them face-down in a pile. The Zookeeper gives one Figure Zoo figure to each player. All the players stand up holding their Figure Zoo figures.

3 The Zookeeper picks the top card and reads it aloud. Each player decides whether his or her figure matches the attribute. If it does not, the player sits down. The Zookeeper picks another card. Play until there is only one figure left. The last player standing is the winner.

4 Choose a different Zookeeper. Trade figures with another group of players. Mix up the cards, and play again. Play as many games as you can. Try to use all the figures in the Figure Zoo.

GAME

Volume Builder

Game Purpose
To practice estimating and finding volume

Materials
- Inch cubes
- Coin
- Scratch paper

Volume Builder

How To Play The Game

1 This game is for two players. The object of the game is to score points by building prisms with the greatest possible volumes.

2 Start by placing a 1-inch cube on a flat surface between you and your partner. The volume of the cube is 1 cubic inch. Decide who will go first. Then take turns.

3 Toss the coin. Heads means 1, and tails means 2.
- If the coin lands on heads, you may add 1 layer horizontally or vertically to the prism.
- If the coin lands on tails, you may add 2 layers horizontally or vertically to the prism.

4 Think about the prism you want to build, and estimate its volume. That will help you decide which direction—horizontal or vertical—will give the prism with the greater volume.
- Add your layer or layers according to the coin toss.
- Compute the volume, and record it on scratch paper. The prism's volume is your score for the round.

5 Take turns. Total your score after each round. The first player to score 200 points wins!

CHALLENGE

Many different nets can be used to make a cube. Only two of the three nets shown below can be folded into a cube. Can you tell which net will not form a cube?

For each net:

- Decide whether it can be folded to make a cube. If it can be folded into a cube, predict which face will be opposite the purple face.

- Test your prediction. Copy the net. Cut it out and fold it to make a cube.

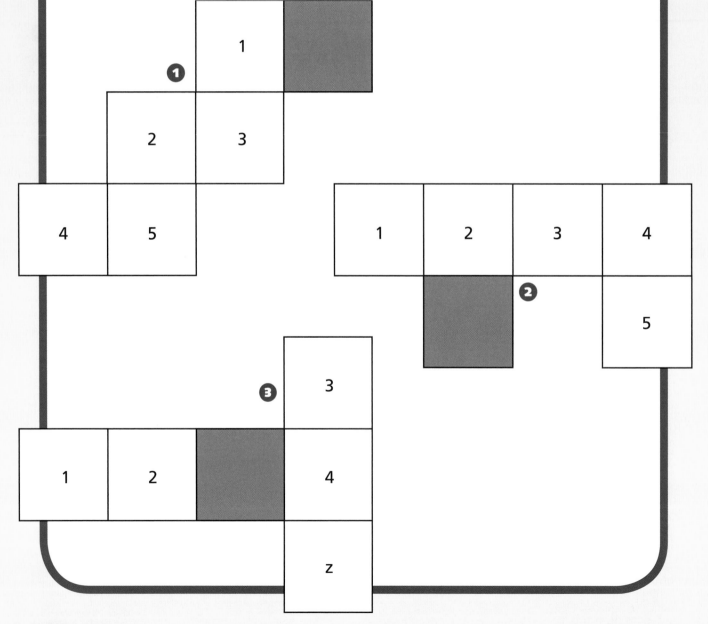

Chapter

12 Extending the Number Line

Dear Student,

The number line is home to many different kinds of numbers. You know how to arrange counting numbers, fractions, and decimals on the number line to show their size. In this chapter, you will be exploring numbers that "live" to the left of 0 on the number line. These numbers are called **negative numbers** and have a minus sign (⁻) in front of them.

You may have used negative numbers in describing temperature. In places where it gets very cold in the winter, people might say, "It was minus 10 out this morning." Negative 10 is farther below zero than negative 5, so ⁻10° is colder than ⁻5°.

In Chapter 9, you measured temperatures using the Fahrenheit system. In this chapter, you will work with the metric temperature system, which is called **Celsius.** In Celsius, water freezes at 0 degrees and boils at 100 degrees. Can you think of situations besides temperatures in which something might go below zero?

Mathematically yours,
The authors of *Think Math!*

THE WORLD ALMANAC FOR KIDS

Fun with Golf

In golf, the person with the lowest score wins. Each golf course has a number assigned to each hole, called par, which depends on the difficulty of the hole. The sum of the numbers for the whole course is par for the entire course.

The scores to the right show the final results for a local golf tournament. The numbers show the golfers' score above or below par for the course.

FACT·ACTIVITY 1

Use the table of golf scores.

1. Copy the number line on a separate sheet of paper. Write the players' names below their scores.

2. Which players had scores above par?

3. Which player's score is farthest to the left on the number line?

4. Who won the golf tournament?

Results of a Local Golf Tournament	
Golfers	Final Score Compared to Par
Ava	$^+5$
Brett	$^-3$
Corey	$^+4$
Dan	$^-5$
Eden	$^+1$

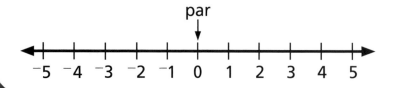

par

$^-5$ $^-4$ $^-3$ $^-2$ $^-1$ 0 1 2 3 4 5

There are either 9 or 18 holes on a golf course. At each hole, golfers try to hit their golf ball as close to the hole on the green as possible, but there are some things that could interfere, such as trees, ponds, and sand traps.

FACT · ACTIVITY 2

Use the grid to answer the questions.

1. Where is the hole located in relation to Kyle's ball?

2. Where is Larry's golf ball located on the coordinate grid?

3. The tree shrubs will be moved for an upcoming tournament. Each corner of the rectangular shrub area will be moved 4 units to the right and 2 units down. What is the new position of the shrub area?

CHAPTER PROJECT

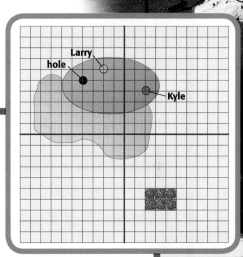

Work with a partner to create your own mini-golf game.

- Draw a coordinate grid with 4 quadrants. Show ⁻5 to 5 on each axis. Then draw features such as waterfalls, barriers, windmills, and trees.

- Indicate the tee, or starting place, and the hole on your grid. Place a game piece on the tee.

- Prepare 2 sets of cards labeled ⁻5 to 5 (including 0) and place them in a bag.

- Pick 2 cards. The first card represents the first number in the ordered pair. The second card represents the second number in the ordered pair. Place your game piece on the coordinates. The player closer to the hole wins.

- Put the cards back in the bag and repeat the game nine times to see who wins the most "holes."

Materials

grid paper

index cards or squares of paper

game pieces (such as pennies and paper clips)

REVIEW MODEL
Understanding Negative Numbers

Sometimes in everyday life, you need to use numbers that are less than zero.

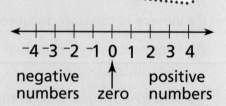

"I had 2 points in a game. Then I drew a card that said, 'You lose 5 points.'"

"The temperature was 3 degrees. That night it fell by 7 degrees."

On a number line, the **negative numbers** are found on the opposite side of zero from the positive numbers. Negative numbers have a minus sign in front of them. Positive numbers may have a plus sign in front, but usually they are written without a sign.

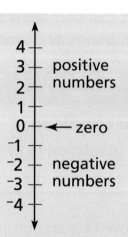

positive numbers

← zero

negative numbers

```
←——+——+——+——+——+——+——+——+——+——→
  ⁻4 ⁻3 ⁻2 ⁻1  0  1  2  3  4
```

negative numbers   zero   positive numbers

To compare numbers, look at their locations on a number line. On a horizontal number line, numbers get greater as you move to the right.

Which is greater, ⁻3 or 1? 1 is farther to the right on a horizontal number line. So, 1 > ⁻3.

On a vertical number line, numbers get greater as you move up.

Which is greater, ⁻1 or ⁻4? ⁻1 is above ⁻4 on a vertical number line. So, ⁻1 > ⁻4.

You can use a number line to solve problems involving negative numbers.

Problem I had 2 points in a game. Then I drew a card that said, "You lose 5 points." How many points did I have then?

Solution Start with 2 points. Jump 5 points backward. You end with ⁻3 points.

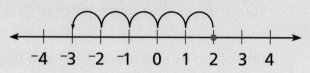

```
←——+——+——+——+——+——+——+——+——+——→
  -4  -3  -2  -1   0   1   2   3   4
```

✔ Check for Understanding

Tell which number is greater.

1 ⁻3 or 0?

2 2 or ⁻5?

3 ⁻1 or ⁻2?

4 4 or 0?

5 The temperature was 3° Celsius. That night it fell by 7° Celsius. What was the final temperature?

REVIEW MODEL
Finding and Identifying Points on a Grid

You can find the location of a given point on a grid by counting spaces. Find the point (4,⁻5).

Step ❶ Start at the **origin**, the place where the horizontal and vertical axes intersect.

Step ❷ Look at the first number in the ordered pair. If it is positive, move right that number of spaces. If it is negative, move left.

Step ❸ Look at the second number in the ordered pair. If it is positive, move up that number of spaces. If it is negative, move down.

Step ❹ Mark the point.

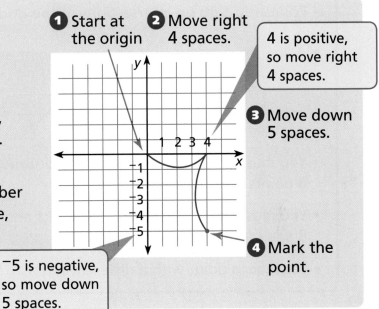

❶ Start at the origin

❷ Move right 4 spaces.

4 is positive, so move right 4 spaces.

❸ Move down 5 spaces.

❹ Mark the point.

⁻5 is negative, so move down 5 spaces.

To identify a point on a grid, find its distances from the two axes. Identify point *P.*

Step ❶ The point is 2 spaces **left** of the vertical axis. The first number is ⁻2. (If the point is **right** of the vertical axis, the first number is positive.)

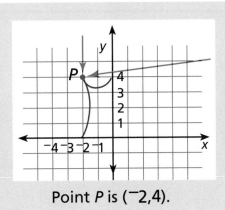

Step ❷ The point is 4 spaces **above** the horizontal axis. The second number is 4. (If the point is **below** the horizontal axis, the second number is negative.)

Point *P* is (⁻2,4).

✔Check for Understanding

Solve.

❶ Where on a grid is the point (⁻2,6)?

❷ What point is 3 spaces right of the vertical axis and 7 spaces above the horizontal axis?

EXPLORE
Can You Copy My Picture?

1 On a blank grid page, make a design with points and line segments, following these rules:

> • Points must go on intersections of the grid.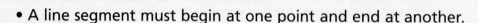
>
> • A line segment must begin at one point and end at another.
>
>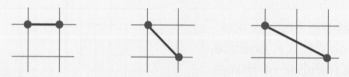
>
> • You must use at least 3 points and not more than 8 points in your design.
>
> • You must use at least 3 line segments and not more than 8 line segments in your design.
>
> • Label each point with a different letter.

2 Write directions explaining how to copy your design onto a blank grid.

> • Use ordered pairs such as (2,3) to describe where to draw points.
>
> • Use the letter labels of the points to describe which points to connect.
>
> $$\overline{AB}$$

3 Exchange sets of directions with a partner. Follow your partner's directions to draw a design on a blank grid, while your partner follows yours.

4 Did you copy your partner's design accurately?

EXPLORE
Changing a Figure's Coordinates

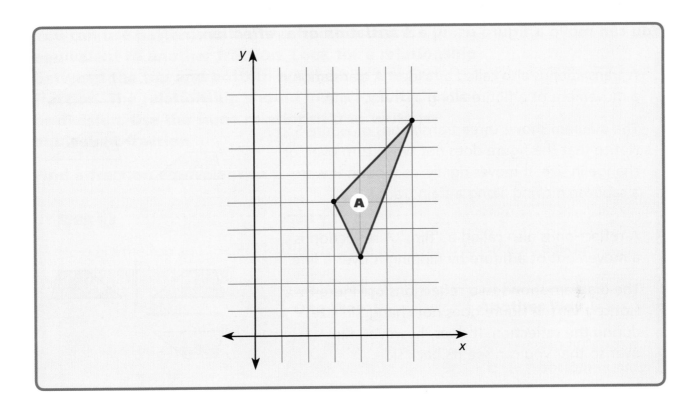

1 What happens to Figure A when you change the
coordinates of all of its points according to the
rules in these tables?

A	B	C	D
(x,y)	$(x + 3,y)$	$(x,y - 2)$	$(x + 6,y + 4)$
(3,5)	(6,5)	(3,3)	(9,9)
(4,3)	(7,3)	(4,1)	(10,7)
(6,8)	(9,8)	(6,6)	(12,12)

2 Use a copy of the Figure Changing Rules Page to
complete the tables and draw Figures B, C, and D.

REVIEW MODEL
Translating and Reflecting Figures

You can move a figure using a *translation* or a *reflection*.

A translation is also called a "slide." A translation is a movement of a figure along a straight line.

The diagram shows three translations of Figure S. Notice that the figure does not twist, turn over, or change in size. It moves rigidly, as though it were a caboose moving along a train track.

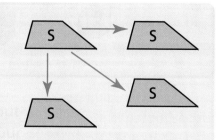

A reflection is also called a "flip." A reflection is a movement of a figure by flipping it over a line.

The diagram shows two reflections of Figure R. Notice that the figure does not change in size during the reflection. It does, however, flip over so that you can see its back side.

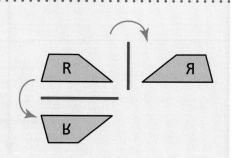

Figures and points can be translated and reflected on a grid.

The diagram shows a translation of Figure A and a reflection of Figure A over the horizontal axis.

Point *K* is one corner of Figure A. It is located at (⁻2,4).

When Figure A is translated, point *K* is translated to (5,1). When Figure A is reflected over the horizontal axis, point *K* is reflected to (⁻2,⁻4).

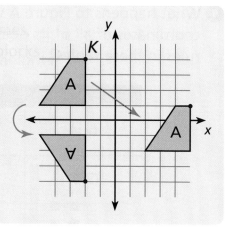

✔Check for Understanding

Tell whether the letter has been translated or reflected.

1   G
        G

2   N
        И

3 The point (⁻5,1) is one corner of Shape A above. Give the coordinates of the point after Shape A is translated and reflected as shown.

EXPLORE
Graphing Number Sentences

There are many pairs of numbers that you could pick for *x* and *y* to make this number sentence true: $y = x + 4$.

Here are some examples:

(x,y)
(1,5)
(2,6)
(3,7)

Each of these pairs of numbers are coordinates of points.

1 Find at least 3 more pairs of numbers that fit $y = x + 4$.

Record them in the first table on the Graphing on a Coordinate Grid Activity Master.

Then draw the point for each pair of coordinates on the grid.

2 Find 5 pairs of numbers that make this sentence true: $y = x + 3$.

Record them in the second table and draw the points on the grid.

3 Using the third table, do the same for this sentence: $y = x + 1$.

4 What do you notice about the three sets of points you graphed?

REVIEW MODEL
Problem Solving Strategy
Draw a Picture

The streets of Hilldale run north and south. They are numbered consecutively, beginning with **1st** Street. The avenues run east and west. They are numbered consecutively, beginning with **1st** Avenue. Anton lives at the corner of **2nd** Street and **4th** Avenue. Tony's Grocery is located at **7th** Street and **2nd** Avenue. Best Grocery is located at **5th** Street and **7th** Avenue. Anton wants to ride his bike from his house to the closest grocery store. Which store should he ride to?

Strategy: Draw a Picture

 Read to Understand

What do you know from reading the problem?

the street and avenue layout of Hilldale, and the locations of Anton's house and two grocery stores

What do you need to find?

the store closest to Anton's house

 Plan

What strategy can you use to solve the problem?

You can *draw a picture*—a map—of Hilldale. Then you can measure the distances from Anton's house to the two stores.

 Solve

How can you solve the problem?

From the given information, I can draw a map of the town, and place dots at Anton's house and the two stores. Then I can find the shortest distance from Anton's house to each store. I must remember that Anton can ride his bike only on streets and avenues, without taking shortcuts. My map shows that the shortest distance to Best Grocery, 6 blocks, is **1** block shorter than the shortest distance to Tony's Grocery. So, Best Grocery is closest.

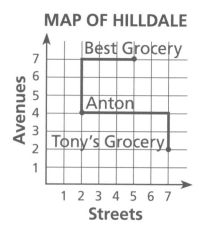

MAP OF HILLDALE

 Check

Look back at the problem. Did you answer the questions that were asked? Does the answer make sense?

Problem Solving Practice

Use the strategy *draw a picture* to solve.

1 Melissa's garden is a square 24 feet on a side. She placed a fence post at every corner and every 6 feet along the sides. How many fence posts did she use?

2 Aaron parked his car in the underground garage in the Seaview Building. Over the next hour he took the elevator up to the ground floor, up another 6 stories, down 4 stories, up 9 stories, down 5 stories, and down 10 stories to his car. On which floor was he parked?

Problem Solving Strategies

✔ Act It Out
✔ **Draw a Picture**
✔ Guess and Check
✔ Look for a Pattern
✔ Make a Graph
✔ Make a Model
✔ Make an Organized List
✔ Make a Table
✔ Solve a Simpler Problem
✔ Use Logical Reasoning
✔ Work Backward
✔ Write an Equation

Mixed Strategy Practice

Use any strategy to solve. Explain.

3 A brick weighs 6 pounds plus half of its total weight. How much does the brick weigh?

4 A baseball team has five pitchers and two catchers. How many different pitcher-catcher combinations are possible?

5 Tomas's house number is a multiple of his age, which is 26. The house number consists of three consecutive digits. What is the number?

6 There are six more girls than boys in the fourth grade. If there are 100 students total, how many boys are there?

7 There are four houses in a row on Digby Street. Marcus lives west of Gregory. Della lives east of Gregory. Taylor lives between Gregory and Della. Who lives farthest west?

8 Val bought three sweaters. The sales tax on her purchase was $4. The total cost, including tax, was $91. If the sweaters were all the same price, what was the cost of each?

9 There are 11 blue guppies and 8 yellow guppies in a fish bowl. They begin jumping one at a time into a second bowl. How many must jump before you can be sure that there are two of the same color in the second bowl?

10 A square rug has an area of 64 square feet. A snail crawled around the outside of the rug at a rate of 2 feet per hour. How long did it take the snail to complete the journey?

Chapter 12 Vocabulary

Choose the best vocabulary term from Word List A for each sentence.

1 The symbol that means subtraction is the ___?___ sign.

2 A(n) ___?___ sign in front of a number means the opposite of that number.

3 A number to the right of zero on the number line is called a(n) ___?___.

4 A pair of numbers used to locate a point on a coordinate plane is a(n) ___?___.

5 The ___?___ of a coordinate plane is where the two axes meet.

6 A straight path that extends in both directions is a(n) ___?___.

7 A(n) ___?___ is the very last point on one side of a line segment.

8 A(n) ___?___ is a part of a line that includes two endpoints and all the points between them.

9 A grid with a horizontal axis and a vertical axis is a(n) ___?___.

Word List A

axes
axis
coordinate
coordinate
 plane
coordinates
endpoint
function
grid
line
line segment
minus
negative
negative
 number
ordered pair
origin
positive
 number

Complete each analogy using the best term from Word List B.

10 A house number is to an address as a coordinate is to a(n) ___?___.

11 A bead is to a necklace as a(n) ___?___ is to a line.

Word List B

axis
function
grid
line segment
ordered pair

Talk Math

Discuss with a partner what you have learned about graphing numbers. Use the vocabulary terms *negative number*, *positive number*, and *origin*.

12 How do you label the axes on a coordinate plane?

13 How do you plot an ordered pair on a coordinate plane?

Concept Map

14 Create a concept map for *Coordinate Plane.* Use what you have learned about the parts of a coordinate plane.

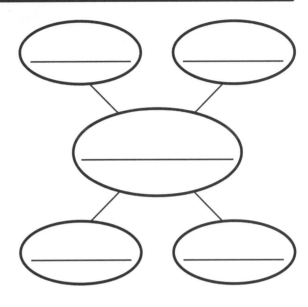

Word Definition Map

15 Create a word definition map for the term *negative number.*

A What is it?

B What is it like?

C What are some examples?

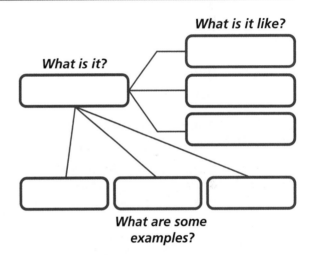

What's in a Word?

FUNCTION The word *function* can describe a job: Sam's *function* is as a team coach. The word *function* can also describe a purpose: The *function* of a dam is to hold back water. *Function* can also describe an event: A PTA open house is a school *function.*

In math, a *function* is a special kind of relationship, in which an output's value depends on an input.

GAME

Freeze or Fry

Game Purpose
To practice adding and subtracting Celsius temperatures

Materials
- Activity Master 131: *Freeze or Fry* game board
- Paper bag
- Number cubes (2 of one color, 2 of another color)
- Small objects to use as game tokens (1 for each player)

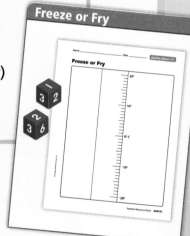

How To Play The Game

1 This is a game for two players. You will need the game board, paper bag, and two sets of number cubes. Each player needs one token.

2 Put the four number cubes in the paper bag. Choose which color will mean a temperature increase and which will mean a temperature decrease.

3 Put your tokens at 0° Celsius. Decide who will go first.

4 Without looking, take two number cubes from the bag. Toss them.
- The colors of the cubes show whether the temperature increases or decreases. The numbers tossed show how many degrees to increase or decrease.
- Combine the result of the toss to find how many degrees, and in which direction, to move your token.

Example: Blue means increase. Green means decrease.

Blue 4 means to increase 4°. Green 1 means to decrease 1°.

So, move your token up a total of 3°.

5 Put the cubes back in the bag for the next player's turn. Play until one player's token goes above the highest temperature or below the lowest temperature on the thermometer.

GAME

Coordinate Hide-and-Seek

Game Purpose
To practice using ordered pairs to name and locate points

Materials
- Activity Master 134: *Blank Grid*
- Small objects to use as game tokens (1 for each player)
- Manila folder

How To Play The Game

Coordinate Hide-and-Seek

1 This is a game for two players. Each player needs one blank grid and one game token. Sit opposite each other. Stand the manila folder between your grids.

2 Secretly place the token on your grid. The token must be placed at an intersection of two grid lines.

3 Take turns guessing the location of the other player's token.
- You may ask only one question on each turn.
- The question must have a *yes* or *no* answer.

These are examples of questions you may ask:
- Is it at (3,4)?
- Is it to the left of (3,4)?
- Is the first coordinate positive?
- Is the second coordinate 3?

Record your responses. You can use counters (in a different color from yours) to track the responses on your grid. Or you can mark the responses directly on your grid.

4 The first player to locate the other player's token is the winner. Play as many games as time allows.

CHALLENGE

Find the missing point or points on each grid. Then write the ordered pair for each point in the figure. Hint: You may want to use a blank grid to draw the figures. There may be more than one answer.

1 Two more points are needed to make a rectangle.

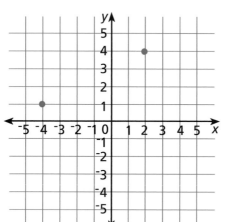

2 One more point is needed to make a right triangle.

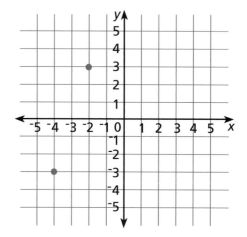

3 Two more points are needed to make a square.

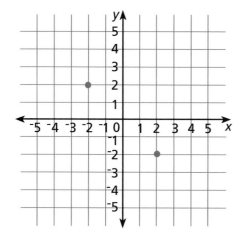

4 Two more points are needed to make a trapezoid.

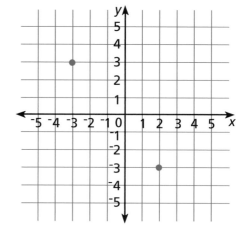

13 Division

Dear Student,

By now you should be very proud that you know so many multiplication facts. You even know about strategies for multiplying larger numbers. In this chapter you'll use all of this knowledge to divide larger numbers.

How can you use multiplication to do division? Well, you already know what a fact family is, so how do you think you can use $12 \times 6 = 72$ to find $72 \div 6$?

How can this picture help you solve this problem?

6 feet

Area = 72 square feet

In this chapter, you'll review and develop your approaches for solving problems like these. Have fun!

Mathematically yours,
The authors of **Think Math!**

Denim Data

In 1873, Jacob Davis and Levi Strauss turned denim, thread, and metal into the most popular clothing product in the world. Although denim work pants had been around since the 1600s, it wasn't until tailor Davis used metal rivets to strengthen points of strain that these pants became popular.

Today, a regular pair of denim jeans has 5 rivets and 5 buttons and requires about $1\frac{3}{4}$ yards of 60-inch wide denim fabric.

FACT·ACTIVITY 1

Use the information above for problems 1–3.

1. Write a multiplication sentence to show how many pairs of denim jeans can be made using 60 rivets.

2. Fabric is usually purchased by the yard. The buyer checks the width of the fabric and then asks for the number of yards desired. Estimate how many pairs of jeans can be made from 135 yards of denim based on 60-inch width fabric? Explain.

3. What if a new style of jeans were made that required 9 rivets per pair? Show how you can find the number of jeans that can be made from 342 rivets. Write the number of jeans you can make.

One bale of cotton weighs about **500** pounds and can make more than **225** pairs of denim jeans.

Answer the questions.

A tailor, Mrs. Elliott, has purchased some yards of 60-inch wide denim to make denim jeans.

1 Mrs. Elliott has **360** inches of denim to make regular denim jeans. If it takes exactly **63** inches of denim to make a pair of men's jeans, will she be able to make 6 pairs of jeans? Use estimation to explain.

2 Mrs. Elliot uses **324** inches of denim to make 6 different styles of women's jeans. If each style requires the same number of inches of denim, how many inches of denim per pair of jeans does she use?

3 About how many bales of cotton are needed to manufacture **925** pairs of jeans?

CHAPTER PROJECT

Some people make quilts from discarded denim jeans. A patchwork quilt can be made from equal-sized square patches of denim sewn together.

- Decide on and draw a design for a rectangular quilt up to 4 feet by 6 feet in size.

- How many inches long will it be? How many inches wide will it be?

- How many equal-sized patches will fit across and down? Try several variations before you decide on one.

- Use division to show the size of each patch in the width and length of your quilt.

- Draw a picture of your final design. You may want to decorate the patches with symbols, letters, or words.

ALMANAC
Fact

Levi Strauss always disliked the term "jeans." The denim work pants were called "waist-high overalls." Not until the mid-1930s did the company ever refer to them as jeans.

EXPLORE
Making Quilts

Andrea is making a quilt with an area of 15 square feet.

Lynn is making a quilt with an area of 35 square feet.

Before they began their quilts, they bought fabric together. Fabric is sold in various lengths, but always with a 5-foot width.

1 What length of fabric should they buy to make both of their quilts? (You may use square tiles to help you answer this question.)

Andrea and Lynn decided to sew their quilts together.

2 Draw a picture of this quilt to find the new length.

3 Write a number sentence to describe the area of the two joined quilts.

What's the length of the new quilt?

EXPLORE
"Missing-Factor" Puzzles

| 0 | 1 | 2 | 4 | 8 | 16 |

Some of these number sentences can be completed using the numbers from the green block above. Copy and complete those sentences.

1

$5 \times \blacksquare = 20$

2

$9 \times \blacksquare = 18$

3

$3 \times \blacksquare = 24$

4

$6 \times \blacksquare = 6$

5

$5 \times \blacksquare = 15$

6

$4 \times \blacksquare = 28$

7 How can you complete the other number sentences using a *sum* of numbers from the green block?

REVIEW MODEL
Finding Missing Factors

You can solve missing-factor problems in several steps. First, look for a multiple of the given factor that is close to but less than the product. Subtract to find how close to the product you were. Repeat the process until you find the missing factor.

Find the missing factor: $16 \times \blacksquare = 208$

Step ❶ Estimate a multiple of 16 that is less than or equal to 208. Try 10, 20, 30, or some other multiple of 10.

Think: $16 \times 1 = 16$, so $16 \times \mathbf{10} = 160$
$16 \times 2 = 32$, so $16 \times \mathbf{20} = 320$
Since 320 is greater than 208, we'll use **10** as the first partial factor.

- -

Step ❷ Subtract the multiple of 16 from 208:

$$\begin{array}{r} 208 \\ -160 \\ \hline 48 \end{array}$$

- -

Step ❸ Estimate or calculate exactly a multiple of 16 that is less than or equal to 48.

Think: $16 \times 1 = 16$, $16 \times 2 = 32$, and $16 \times 3 = 48$
Since 48 is equal to 48, we'll use **3** as the second partial factor.

- -

Step ❹ Subtract the multiple of 16 from 48:

$$\begin{array}{r} 48 \\ -48 \\ \hline 0 \end{array}$$

- -

Step ❺ Repeat the steps. When you find a difference of zero, add the partial products. $10 + 3 = 13$, so $16 \times 13 = 208$

✔Check for Understanding

Find the missing factor.

❶ $18 \times \blacksquare = 288$

❷ $12 \times \blacksquare = 288$

❸ $\blacksquare \times 25 = 775$

❹ $\blacksquare \times 34 = 510$

❺ $23 \times \blacksquare = 759$

❻ $\blacksquare \times 42 = 882$

EXPLORE
A Division Story

The area of Angi's lawn is 126 square feet. The lawn is rectangular and 7 feet wide.

Angi wants to buy sod to plant her lawn with grass. The garden store she goes to sells sod in 1-foot by 1-foot squares.

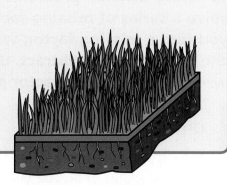

1 Draw a picture to represent this situation.

2 How long is Angi's lawn?

3 How many square feet of sod should Angi buy?

REVIEW MODEL
Recording Division Steps

To record division problems using the new format, solve a series of missing-factor problems. Each time you find a missing factor, write it in two places in the format. Then subtract. Use the difference to write a new missing factor problem.

Divide: 168 ÷ 6

Step ❶ Draw the division "box." Write the number **you are dividing** inside. Write the number **you are dividing by** outside.

Step ❷ Find the greatest factor that is a multiple of 10 with a product less than 168. Write it (**20**) here and above 168, as shown.

Step ❸ Subtract. Write the difference (**48**) here.

Step ❹ Find a factor with a product less than or equal to the difference (**48**). Write it (**5**) here and above 168, as shown.

Step ❺ Subtract. Write the difference (**18**) here.

Step ❻ Find a factor with a product less than the difference (**18**). Write it (**3**) here and above 168, as shown.

Step ❼ Continue until the difference is zero.

$$\begin{array}{r} 3 \\ 5 \\ 20 \\ 6\,\overline{)\,168} \end{array}$$

$6 \times \boxed{20} = \underline{120}$

$\boxed{48}$

$6 \times \boxed{5} = \underline{30}$

$\boxed{18}$

$6 \times \boxed{3} = \underline{18}$

$\boxed{0}$

Step ❽ Add the factors: 20 + 5 + 3 = 28, so 168 ÷ 6 = 28.

In Steps 4 and 6, many different factors are possible. In the example above, the factors 5 and 3 are shown, but others are possible.

✔Check for Understanding

Find the quotient.

❶ 136 ÷ 8   **❷** 110 ÷ 5   **❸** 189 ÷ 7   **❹** 306 ÷ 9

Exploring Division

Without solving any of these problems, decide
which problem has the smallest answer and
which problem has the largest answer.

$$808 \div 8 = \blacksquare$$

$$590 \div 10 = \blacksquare$$

$$87 \div 1 = \blacksquare$$

$$234 \div 9 = \blacksquare$$

$$84 \div 4 = \blacksquare$$

$$33 \div 33 = \blacksquare$$

How did you decide?

Gina is painting a fence with **150** posts. When she has painted three times as many posts as she has already painted, she'll have **12** more posts to paint. How many posts has she painted?

Strategy: Work Backward

 Read to Understand

What do you know from reading the problem?

There are **150** fence posts. When Gina has painted three times as many posts as she has already painted, she'll have just **12** more to paint.

What do you need to find out?

the number of fence posts that Gina has painted

 Plan

How can you solve this problem?

You could use the information in the problem to work backward from the end to the beginning.

 Solve

How can you work backward to solve the problem?

Think: At the end, Gina will have painted **150** posts.

Just before that, she painted the last **12** posts. That means she must have painted $150 - 12 = 138$ posts before that.

138 posts is three times the number of posts she has already painted. So, she must have painted **138** ÷ **3** posts so far.

$138 ÷ 3 = 46$

So, Gina must have painted **46** posts so far.

 Check

Look back at the problem. Did you answer the questions that were asked? Does the answer make sense?

Problem Solving Practice

Problem Solving Strategies

✔ Act It Out
✔ Draw a Picture
✔ Guess and Check
✔ Look for a Pattern
✔ Make a Graph
✔ Make a Model
✔ Make an Organized List
✔ Make a Table
✔ Solve a Simpler Problem
✔ Use Logical Reasoning
✔ **Work Backward**
✔ Write an Equation

Use the strategy *work backward* to solve.

1 Brittany wants to save $400 for her vacation. When she has saved four times as much as she has saved already, she will need only $72 more. How much has she saved?

2 Dennis, Vicky, and Beth divided up the houses in their neighborhood to conduct a survey. Dennis interviewed the owners of half the houses. Vicky interviewed the owners of one-third of the houses that remained. Beth interviewed the 12 remaining owners. How many houses were in the neighborhood?

Mixed Strategy Practice

Use any strategy to solve. Explain.

3 Anton bought 33 apples and bananas. He bought 7 more bananas than apples. How many apples did he buy?

4 The area of a rectangular garden is 36 square yards. Its width is 4 yards. What is its perimeter?

5 There are four candidates for class president. In how many different orders can they stand in a line to have their photos taken?

6 A rectangular rug measures 2 yards by 3 yards. What is the area of the rug is square *feet?*

7 Sunday's temperature was 6 degrees higher than Saturday's. On Monday the temperature fell 11 degrees. On Tuesday it rose 17 degrees to 46 degrees. What was the temperature on Saturday?

8 Peaches cost $2.10 a pound. Apples cost $1.55 a pound. Each week the price of peaches goes down $0.08 a pound and the price of apples goes up $0.03 a pound. How much will each cost when their prices are the same?

9 At a book sale, Annie bought five hardcover books at $3 apiece, and some paperbacks at $2 apiece. She spent $27. How many paperbacks did she buy?

10 Jodie has a penny, a nickel, and a dime. How many different values can she make using one, two, or three coins?

Choose the best vocabulary term from Word List A for each sentence.

1 The number that is to be divided in a division problem is the ___?___.

2 The number that divides the dividend is the ___?___.

3 The ___?___ is the result of multiplication.

4 To replace a number with another number that tells about how many or how much is to ___?___ a number.

5 A set of related multiplication and division equations is a(n) ___?___.

6 The process of finding the total number of items in equal-sized groups is called ___?___.

7 Numbers that are easy to compute mentally are called ___?___.

Word List A

compatible numbers

dividend

divisor

fact family

factor

multiple

multiplication

product

quotient

round

Complete each analogy using the best term from Word List B.

8 Addend is to addition as ___?___ is to multiplication.

9 Product is to multiplication as ___?___ is to division.

Word List B

divisor

estimate

factor

quotient

🗨Talk Math

Discuss with a partner what you have learned about multiplication and division. Use the vocabulary terms *factor* and *product*.

10 How can you solve a missing-factor problem?

11 How can you write a missing-factor problem as a division problem?

12 Suppose you have a missing-factor problem and you know that the missing factor is greater than 10. How can you estimate the missing factor?

Venn Diagram

13 Create a Venn diagram for multiplication and division terms. Use the terms *dividend, divisor, fact family, factor, product,* and *quotient.*

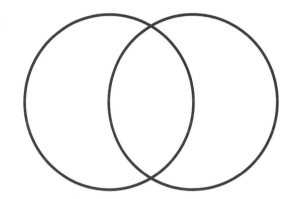

Tree Diagram

14 Create a tree diagram using the terms *operations, addition, subtraction, multiplication,* and *division.* Use what you know and what you have learned about the operations.

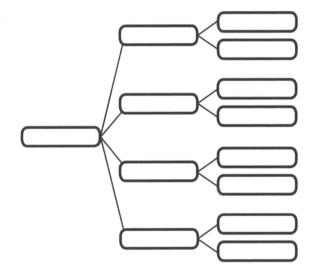

What's in a Word?

ESTIMATE The word *estimate* can be a verb or a noun. The verb usually means to round numbers before computing with them. The noun means the sum, difference, product, or quotient of the rounded numbers. A house painter might *estimate* the cost of supplies needed to paint a house. Then the painter will give an *estimate* of the total cost to paint the house.

GAME

Greatest Factors

Game Purpose
To explore strategies for finding missing factors efficiently

Materials
• Activity Masters:
  Greatest Factors Games I–III

How To Play The Game

1 This is a game for two players. The goal is to collect points by choosing large factors of given numbers. Each game has four puzzles. Take turns choosing which puzzle to use. The player who does not choose the puzzle gets to go first.

2 You are trying to reach the starting number. Take turns filling in the steps. To fill in a step, choose a factor from the large block. Write it in the hexagonal box to complete the multiplication sentence. Tell how much is left.

• If you are filling in the first step, the amount left is the difference between the starting number and the product from the multiplication sentence.

• After the first step, the amount left is the difference between the previous step and the new product.

• If the chosen factor is too large and would give a negative number, do not do the subtraction.

3 Each player earns points equal to the factor chosen from the large block. But if your chosen factor was too large, you get zero points. Keep track of your points on scratch paper.

4 Once the amount left is zero, the remaining steps must use zero as the missing factor. No one gets any points for those steps.

5 After you have filled in all four puzzles, add up your points. The player with more points is the winner.

The Greatest Answer

> **Game Purpose**
> To practice estimating quotients
>
> **Materials**
> • Activity Master: Greatest Answer
> • Activity Master: Score Page

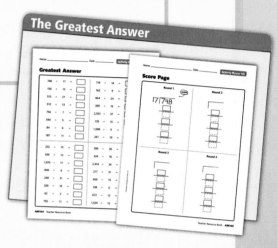

How To Play The Game

1 This is a game for two players. The object is to estimate which problems in four sets of division problems have the largest quotients. Together, choose one of the four sets of division problems.

2 One player uses estimation to choose a division problem with a large quotient from the set. Then the second player chooses a division problem in the same way.

• Solve your division problem.

• Check the other player's work.

• Your score is the answer to the problem. Record your score on the Score Page.

3 Choose one of the remaining sets and repeat Step 2, with the second player choosing a problem first this time. Record your scores.

4 After you have played four rounds, with each player completing one problem from each set, add up all your points. The player with more points is the winner.

CHALLENGE

Albert Einstein was a famous twentieth-century mathematician. Solve the puzzle below to find the word that is missing from this quote by Einstein.

____?____ is more important than knowledge.

1 Estimate or find each quotient exactly.

N   210 ÷ 5

I   324 ÷ 2

A   52 ÷ 4

I   62 ÷ 62

N   624 ÷ 2

T   444 ÷ 4

G   63 ÷ 3

I   174 ÷ 6

O   630 ÷ 3

A   300 ÷ 5

M   48 ÷ 6

2 Order the quotients from least to greatest.

3 Spell out the missing word by matching each letter to the correct quotient. What is the missing word?

14 Algebraic Thinking

Dear Student,

Try this number puzzle:

Did other students also get 1? If not, tell them that they must have made a mistake. That will surprise them!

In this chapter, you will learn how such puzzles work and have a chance to make up your own "think of a number" puzzles. When you do, try them out on your friends and family. See if they can figure out the "tricks" of these puzzles.

Have fun puzzling through this chapter!

Mathematically yours,
The authors of *Think Math!*

- ☑ Think of a number.
- ☑ Add 3 to it.
- ☑ Double your result.
- ☑ Subtract 4.
- ☑ Divide your result by 2.
- ☑ Subtract the number you thought of first.

Aha! Your result is 1!

Model Trains: More Than Just Toys

The Great Train Story is a famous 3,500 square foot model railroad exhibit at the Museum of Science and Industry in Chicago, Illinois. It has 34 trains running along 1,425 feet of track between the miniature cities of Chicago and Seattle. At night, 80,000 windows and 1,291 streetlights light up the scene.

Copy the puzzle below on a piece of paper. If you follow the steps, the last line of the puzzle reveals some interesting facts about the Great Train Story.

Operations \ Facts	A Gallons of glue used	B Height of Sears Tower (feet)	C Number of people worked on this model	D Pounds of dirt used on layout
Start with a number.	47			
Add 5.		16		
Multiply by 2.			84	
Subtract 4.				1,200
Divide by 2.				

FACT·ACTIVITY 1

Complete the puzzle and the sentences below.

A ■ gallons of glue were used.

B ■ feet is the height of the Sears Tower in the model.

C ■ people worked on the project.

D ■ pounds of dirt were used on the layout.

Ernesto and Sally are having a discussion about the *mysterious x*. They have come up with several ways to use *x* in the puzzle in Fact Activity 1.

For 1–4, replace the starting number in each column with *x*. Write the shorthand notation.

1 Use *x* to write an expression for a number in the "Add 5." row.

2 What is the shorthand notation for a number in the "Multiply by 2." row?

3 Use *x* to write an expression for a number in the "Subtract 4." row.

4 What is the shorthand notation for a number in the "Divide by 2." row?

CHAPTER PROJECT

Materials: small empty boxes (tissue or shoe box), paint, construction paper, yarn, glue

Collect empty cardboard boxes to build a link of trains. To link the trains together, pierce 2 holes on one end of each box. Feed a strand of yarn through the holes and secure by tying knots. For the wheels, cut out round pieces of cardboard and glue them on the sides of the train. Paint or glue construction paper to your train to create features such as windows, door handles, and ladders.

- Keep track of the materials you used. How many boxes, wheels, windows, etc. are there?

- Write down clues for your partner to solve the mystery numbers of your train. Your clues must include 3 operations. You must also provide a final number so that your partner will work the clues backward to find the mystery number.

- Write the algebraic expression for each step.

- Finally, have your partner count the pieces from your model to verify the answers.

ALMANAC
Fact

Model railroads began as a hobby in the 1840s. One of the largest model railroads is Northlandz in Flemington, New Jersey. It has more than 100 trains that run on 8 miles of track.

EXPLORE
Number Puzzle Mystery

Ryan discovered a number puzzle where the
directions for each step are given as a picture.

		A	B	C	D	E
Step **1**	🛍	9	■	■	■	■
Step **2**	🛍🛍	?	?	?	?	?
Step **3**	🛍🛍 •••	?	?	?	?	?
Step **4**	🛍 •••	12	5	27	3	16

1 What are the starting numbers for each round of
this puzzle?

2 Describe a single step for getting from the starting
number to the final number.

3 Describe a single step for getting from the final number
to the starting number.

REVIEW MODEL
Using Bags and Counters

You can use bags and counters to create number puzzles, and to see how number puzzles work. When you work a number puzzle, you can add, subtract, multiply, and divide bags and counters as though they were whole numbers.

Example

What the puzzle says:	Joe's number	Taylor's Number	Bags and counters
Think of a number.	7	15	
Double it.	$7 \times 2 = 14$	$15 \times 2 = 30$	
Add 10.	$14 + 10 = 24$	$30 + 10 = 40$	
Divide by 2.	$24 \div 2 = 12$	$40 \div 2 = 20$	
Subtract 3.	$12 - 3 = 9$	$20 - 3 = 17$	

The last picture shows that no matter what number you start with, you will end with the same number plus 2 more. Joe started with 7 and ended with $7 + 2 = 9$. Taylor started with 15 and ended with $15 + 2 = 17$.

✔Check for Understanding

On a separate sheet of paper, draw bags and counters to represent the following four steps in a number puzzle.

1 Think of a number.

2 Add 3.

3 Double it.

4 Subtract 5.

5 Think of a number.

6 Double it.

7 Add 6.

8 Subtract 2.

REVIEW MODEL
Using Shorthand Notation

When a number puzzle says, "Think of a number and double it," it's easy to work the puzzle with bags: 🜲🜲. But suppose the puzzle says, "Think of a number and multiply it by 50." Would you like to draw 50 bags? There's an easier way to work number puzzles.

- Use x or another variable instead of 🜲.
- Use whole numbers to represent the numbers of bags and counters.

	Bags and Counters	Shorthand Notation
Think of a number.	🜲	x
Multiply it by 8.	🜲🜲🜲🜲🜲🜲🜲🜲	$8x$
Add 14.	🜲🜲🜲🜲🜲🜲🜲🜲 ••••• ••••	$8x + 14$
Divide by 2.	🜲🜲🜲🜲 •••• •••	$4x + 7$
Subtract 3.	🜲🜲🜲🜲 ••••	$4x + 4$

✓ Check for Understanding

Use shorthand notation to write the four steps of a number puzzle.

1 **A** Think of a number.   **B** Multiply it by 20.   **C** Add 48.   **D** Divide by 2.

2 **A** Think of a number.   **B** Multiply it by 100.   **C** Subtract 20.   **D** Divide by 4.

EXPLORE
Finding Your Number

Words	Shorthand	Betty	Ted	Jun	Karina
Think of a number.	x	?	?	?	?
Step ❶	$x + 6$	10		21	
Step ❷	$x + 2$	6			2
Step ❸	$2x + 4$	12	26		

❶ What number did each student think of? Use base-ten
blocks or counters to help you.

❷ Use words to describe **Step 1** of this puzzle.

❸ Use words to describe **Step 2** of this puzzle.

❹ Use words to describe **Step 3** of this puzzle.

EXPLORE
Product Near Square Numbers

The 4th graders are making a class flag.
They want its area to be as big as possible.
Their teacher offers them some choices for
the sizes of their flags.

Which should they choose? Why?

1

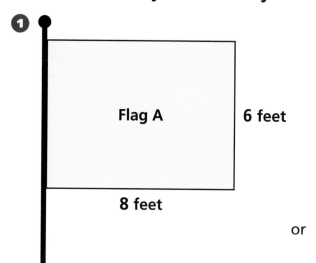

Flag A

6 feet

8 feet

or

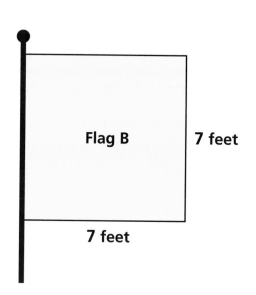

Flag B

7 feet

7 feet

---

2 Flag A is **15-by-17 feet**   or   Flag B is **16-by-16 feet**

---

3 Flag A is **28-by-30 feet**   or   Flag B is **29-by-29 feet**

What do you notice?

REVIEW MODEL
Applying a Squaring Pattern

You can use an amazing number pattern to help you multiply large numbers. The pattern uses the *square* of a number (the number multiplied by itself) and the *nearest neighbors* of the number.

Example 1

number: 7 → square of number: $7 \times 7 = \boxed{49}$

nearest neighbors: 6 and 8 → product of nearest neighbors: $6 \times 8 = \boxed{48}$

Example 2

number: 12 → square of number: $12 \times 12 = \boxed{144}$

nearest neighbors: 11 and 13 → product of nearest neighbors: $11 \times 13 = \boxed{143}$

Notice that in both examples, the square of the number is 1 more than the product of its nearest neighbors.

Example 3

Use mental math to find the product 49×51.

$50 \times 50 = 2{,}500.$

So, $49 \times 51 = 2{,}500 - 1 = 2{,}499.$

> **Think:** The square of 50 is 1 more than the product of 49 and 51.

Example 4

If $73 \times 75 = 5{,}475$, what is 74×74?

$73 \times 75 = 5{,}475.$

So, $74 \times 74 = 5{,}475 + 1 = 5{,}476.$

> **Think:** The square of 74 is 1 more than the product of 73 and 75.

✔Check for Understanding

Use mental math to find the product.

1 19×21 **2** 39×41 **3** 79×81 **4** 99×101

Solve.

5 If $36 \times 38 = 1{,}368$, what is 37×37? **6** If $47 \times 49 = 2{,}303$, what is 48×48?

REVIEW MODEL
Problem Solving Strategy
Work Backward

Kyle bought two tickets to the Spring Concert. The total cost of the tickets, including a $3 service charge, was $39. The equation $2x + 3 = 39$ represents the total cost of the tickets. How can you solve the equation to find the cost of one ticket?

Strategy: Work Backward

Read to Understand

What do you know from reading the problem?

Kyle bought 2 tickets. The service charge was $3. The total cost was $39. The equation $2x + 3 = 39$ represents the total cost.

What do you need to find out?

the price of a ticket

Plan

How can you solve this problem?

You could work backward to solve the equation $2x + 3 = 39$. The value of x will be the cost of one ticket.

Solve

How can you find the value of x in the equation?

If $2x + 3 = 39$, then 39 must be 3 *more than* $2x$. That makes sense, because $39 is $3 more than the cost of two tickets, due to the $3 service charge. So, working backward, $2x$ must be 3 *less than* 39, or 36. If $2x = 36$, then 36 is 2 *times x*. That means that x must be 36 *divided by* 2, or 18. So, the cost of one ticket is $18.

Check

Look back at the problem. Did you answer the questions that were asked? Does the answer make sense?

The answer makes sense because the total cost of 2 tickets (2 × $18 = $36) plus a $3 service charge ($36 + $3 = $39) is $39.

Problem Solving Practice

Use the strategy *work backward* to solve.

1 Damon bought 6 apples and 5 peaches. He spent a total of $4.15. Each apple cost $0.40. How much did each peach cost if all the peaches were the same price?

2 Hallie walks to school from her house by walking 3 blocks north, 4 blocks west, and 1 block south. She walks home by the same route. Describe the route that she follows home.

Problem Solving Strategies

✔ Act It Out
✔ Draw a Picture
✔ Guess and Check
✔ Look for a Pattern
✔ Make a Graph
✔ Make a Model
✔ Make an Organized List
✔ Make a Table
✔ Solve a Simpler Problem
✔ Use Logical Reasoning
✔ **Work Backward**
✔ Write an Equation

Mixed Strategy Practice

Use any strategy to solve. Explain.

3 A photograph has a width of 8 inches and a perimeter of 36 inches. What is its area?

4 How many squares are in the figure at the right?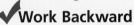

5 The Sharks soccer team played 28 games. Five games ended in ties. The team won 5 more games than it lost. How many games did it win?

6 Mark mows his lawn every 6 days and waters his lawn every 4 days. He watered and mowed on July 1. When was the next day he watered and mowed on the same day?

7 Amber, Michael, and Josh are students. One is in 3rd grade, one is in 4th, and one is in 5th. Michael is not in 5th grade. The 3rd grader is on the track team with Amber and in the chorus with Michael. Which student is in 4th grade?

8 Chelsea's flight to Chicago leaves at 8:20 A.M. She wants to be at the airport 1 hour 45 minutes early. It will take her 45 minutes to drive to the airport. What time should she leave her house?

9 A number cube measures 2 inches on a side. An empty box is cube-shaped and measures 4 inches on a side. How many number cubes can you pack in the box?

10 A donut-frosting machine can frost 6 donuts every 5 seconds. How many donuts can it frost in 1 minute?

Choose the best vocabulary term from Word List A for each sentence.

Word List A

algebra
dot
equation
parentheses
square
variable
x
y
z

1 A study of number patterns with symbols is called ___?___.

2 The most commonly used variable is ___?___.

3 A letter or symbol that stands for one or more numbers is called a(n) ___?___.

4 A(n) ___?___ is a number sentence that shows that two quantities are equal.

5 In algebra, a raised ___?___ between two numbers means to multiply those two numbers.

6 Symbols used to show which operation or operations in a expression should be done first are called ___?___.

7 The product of a number and itself is called the ___?___ of the number.

Complete each analogy using the best term from Word List B.

Word List B

algebra
dot
equation
variable
y

8 A plus sign is to addition as a(n) ___?___ is to multiplication.

9 Sentence is to language as ___?___ is to algebra.

10 Number is to 7 as ___?___ is to *x*.

Talk Math

Discuss with a partner what you have learned about algebra. Use the vocabulary terms *equation* and *variable*.

11 How can you record a number puzzle that works for all numbers?

12 How can you use symbols to represent a square number?

13 Create an analysis chart for the terms *algebra, equation, variable,* and *square.* Use what you know and what you have learned about algebra and rules.

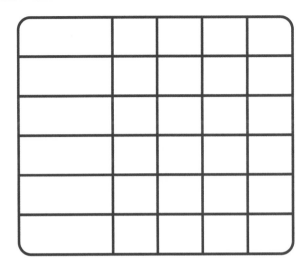

Word Web

14 Create a word web using the word *square.*

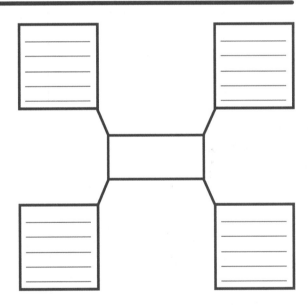

What's in a Word?

ALGEBRA In the ninth century, a Persian mathematician named Abu Ja'far Muhammad ibn Musa al-Khwarizmi wrote a book about math that described algebra. The book was called *The Compendious Book on Calculation by Completing and Balancing.* He wrote the book in Arabic. The word *completing* in the title is *al-jabr* in Arabic. *Al-jabr* became *algebra* in English.

GAME

Make a Puzzle

Game Purpose
To gain further experience with the math behind number puzzles and the strategy *work backward*

Materials
- Activity Masters 147, 148, 149
- counters
- scissors

How To Play The Game

1 This is a game for two players. The object is to make and solve puzzles. Each player will need a *Make a Puzzle* game board. Cut out each set of *Make a Puzzle* cards and place the cards face down.

2 Take turns picking an operation card and a number card. For each pair of cards, record the step in a blank under "Draw a number" on the game board. Fill in the first five blanks above the heavy line. You may mix up each set of cards again at any time.

3 Next, take turns picking a number card. Write the number in the first blank beside "Draw a number." Use that number as the starting number in a puzzle. Work downward through the five steps. You may use counters to help. Complete all your puzzles.

4 Now, write 1, 2, or 3 rules to try to get back your original numbers. If you do not need a row on the game sheet, leave it blank.

5 Complete your puzzles. If you cannot complete any arithmetic because it would mean an uneven division or lead to a negative number, stop working in that column.

6 Find the difference between the original and last number recorded in each column. Add all the differences. The sum is your score. Whoever has fewer points wins.

GAME

Equation Maze

Game Purpose
To practice finding the value of *x* in number sentences written in shorthand notation

Materials
- Activity Masters 150 and 151
- game token
- scissors

How To Play The Game

1 This is a game for two players. The goal is to be the first player through the *Equation Maze.* Cut out all the cards. Place them face down in a stack.

2 Put your game tokens at the start of the maze. Decide who will go first, and then take turns.

3 Pick a card. Find the value of *x*.

- If the value of *x* matches a number in a circle that is connected to the circle where you are, move your token to the new circle.
- If the value of *x* matches more than one circle connected to yours, move your token to either circle.
- If the value of *x* does not match a circle connected to yours, do not move your token.

Examples: Mitzi is at Start. The value of *x* is 10.
    Mitzi can move forward.

    Jin is at 22. The value of *x* is 3.
    Jin has two choices.

    Mitzi is at 27. The value of *x* is 22.
    Mitzi must stay where she is.

4 Play until one player reaches the end of the maze. That player is the winner.

CHALLENGE

Here are two algebra tricks you can try on your family or friends. Before you try them on someone else, test them yourself so you see how they work. Look for a pattern in each trick.

Hint: Try using a variable. That will help you understand how the tricks work.

Algebra Trick #1

☑ Choose any number from 1 to 10.

☑ Add 5 to the number.

☑ Multiply the result by 2.

☑ Subtract 10.

☑ Divide the result by 2.

What number are you left with?

Algebra Trick #2

☑ Choose any number from 1 to 10.

☑ Multiply the number by 2.

☑ Add 2 to the result.

☑ Multiply the result by 2.

☑ Divide the result by 4.

☑ Subtract 1 from the result.

What number are you left with?

❶ Now that you have seen how these two tricks work, do you think they will work with any starting number? Explain.

❷ Make up an algebra trick of your own. Test it to be sure it works. Then try it on someone else.

Chapter

15 Estimation

Dear Student,

Congratulations on making it to the final chapter!

This chapter is all about estimating. You will be estimating lengths, areas, capacities, and money. In what kinds of situations might you estimate? What units might you estimate these things with? What things might you estimate the length, area, or capacity of? What tools could you use to check your estimates?

You will find answers to all of these questions. As you do, we hope you will learn to value estimating and use it to simplify computations in everyday life.

Mathematically yours,
The authors of *Think Math!*

Bee-havior

In a natural beehive, the working bees build honeycombs attached to each other from top to bottom. These honeycombs are made of beeswax and they form hexagonal cells. It takes about 15 pounds of beeswax to form the entire structure of the honeycomb. The cells of the honeycomb are used for storing honey and raising the young.

FACT·ACTIVITY 1

Look at the honeycomb.

1 cm²

1 Estimate the perimeter and area of the honeycomb. Use the fact that the picture of the bee to the right of the honeycomb is 1 square centimeter.

For 2–3, use the drawing.

2 How far does a bee have to fly from the beehive to reach the flowerbed?

3 About how far is the boy from the beehive?

beehive   flowerbed   13 meters

20 meters

A single bee hive can have more than **30,000** bees and produce about **300** pounds of honey in a year. During their lives, 12 worker bees will gather only 1 teaspoon of honey.

FACT·ACTIVITY 2

❶ Suppose the capacity of a jar is **8** ounces. How many jars will you need to hold 1 gallon of honey?

❷ An American consumes about **594** grams (1.31 pounds) of honey per year. Estimate the amount of honey one person will consume in **5** years. Explain how you found your answer.

❸ About how much honey is produced by a colony of bees in a year, in kilograms? Explain.

❹ One gallon of honey weighs about 12 pounds. Estimate how many gallons of honey a single hive can produce in a year.

CHAPTER PROJECT

- Use your new knowledge of bees and honey to estimate how many bees it takes to produce the honey for this recipe.

- Suppose you were to make enough servings of this snack for everyone in your class. Estimate how much more honey you will need for a recipe large enough for everyone in your class.

- Does $\frac{1}{2}$ cup honey weigh the same as $\frac{1}{2}$ cup water? Measure $\frac{1}{2}$ cup of each into identical paper cups and weigh each one. Record your results. Then try other liquids, such as olive oil or juice. Weigh $\frac{1}{2}$ cup of each. Make a chart to show the results. Does the same volume of different liquids weigh the same? Explain.

Honey Snacks

Makes 8 servings:

$1\frac{1}{3}$ cups toppings: ground toasted almonds, ground coconut, candy sprinkles, or graham cracker crumbs

4 just-ripe bananas, peeled

$\frac{1}{2}$ cup honey

8 popsicle sticks

Combine one or more toppings in a mixing bowl to make $1\frac{1}{3}$ cups. Slice each banana in half crosswise. Insert a popsicle stick into each half banana. Spread honey on each banana to coat evenly. Roll each banana half in the toppings to coat.

ALMANAC Fact

Honey bees fly up to 24 km/hr (15 mph) and their wings beat 200 times/sec (12,000 beats/min).

EXPLORE
The Lemonade Stand

Five friends set up a lemonade stand by the side of the road. They sold cups of lemonade for 10¢ each and cookies for 25¢ each.

They earned $8.15 on Saturday and $9.65 on Sunday. They decided that they should each get $4.00.

1 Why won't this work?

2 How much should each friend get?

EXPLORE
Estimating Perimeter

Paul Perimeter is $1\frac{1}{4}$ meters tall. His pencil is a little more than 10 centimeters long.

Paul is going to glue a border around the sides of his door. He is trying to find the door's perimeter to figure out how much border he needs.

1 How can Paul use his height to estimate the perimeter in meters?

2 How can Paul use his pencil to estimate the perimeter of the door in centimeters?

3 Would these two estimates of the door's perimeter make sense? Why or why not?

4 times Paul's height   100 pencils

REVIEW MODEL
Finding Perimeter and Area

The *perimeter* of a figure is the distance around the outside. The *area* of a figure is the number of square units on the inside.

perimeter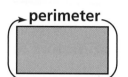

area

Example 1
Find the perimeter of the rectangle.

7 in.

4 in.

One Way ·

Add the lengths of the four sides.
4 in. + 7 in. + 4 in. + 7 in. = 22 in.

The perimeter is 22 in.

Another Way · · · · · · · · · · · · · · · · · · ·

Add two adjacent sides:
4 in. + 7 in. = 11 in.

Multiply the sum by 2:
11 in. × 2 = 22 in.

Example 2
Find the area of the rectangle.

9 ft

3 ft

One Way ·

Count the number of square units inside. There are 27 squares.

9 ft

3 ft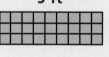

The area is 27 sq ft.

Another Way · · · · · · · · · · · · · · · · · · ·

Multiply the length by the width.

9 ft × 3 ft = 27 sq ft.

The area is 27 sq ft.

✔Check for Understanding

Find the perimeter and area of each rectangle.

1

5 in.

3 in.

2

6 cm

2 cm

3

8 ft

3 ft

EXPLORE
Comparing Liters and Gallons

Felisha is going to the beach and wants to bring lots of water with her. She has two water coolers. One of the coolers holds **1 gallon** and the other holds **4 liters**.

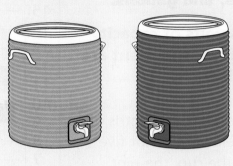

1 What can Felisha do to figure out which cooler holds more water?

2 Felisha just remembered that 1 liter is a little bit more than 1 quart. How can this help her decide which cooler is bigger?

3 Felisha changed her mind. She wants to bring lemonade instead of water to the beach. To make lemonade, she mixes one lemonade packet with **8 cups of water**. About how many packets should she use to make enough lemonade to fill the larger cooler? Explain your reasoning.

REVIEW MODEL
Comparing Units of Capacity

The *capacity* of a three-dimensional object is the amount that it can hold.

The four most common units of capacity in the customary system of measurement are cups, pints, quarts, and gallons.

The two most common units of capacity in the metric system of measurement are the milliliter and the liter.

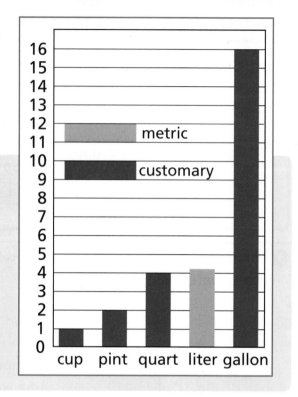

In the diagram at the right, the lengths of the bars indicate the relative sizes of five of the six basic units—the cup, the pint, the quart, the liter, and the gallon.

The sixth unit, the milliliter, is too small to appear on the diagram. It is only $\frac{1}{236}$ as big as a cup.

Notice that a liter is slightly bigger than a quart.

Examples

A How many pints are in a gallon?

> The gallon bar is 8 times the height of the pint bar, so there are 8 pints in a gallon.

B Which is bigger, a gallon or 4 liters?

> Since a liter is bigger than a quart, 4 liters is bigger than 4 quarts. Since there are 4 quarts in a gallon, 4 liters is bigger than a gallon.

C Which is bigger, a pint or 500 milliliters?

> A pint is 2 cups.
> There are 236 milliliters in a cup.
> So a pint is 2 × 236 = 472 milliliters, which is smaller than 500 milliliters.

✔Check for Understanding

Solve.

1 How many cups are in a quart?

2 Which is bigger, 3 pints or a liter?

3 How many quarts are in a half-gallon?

4 Which is bigger, 900 milliliters or 4 cups?

5 Which is bigger, 5 cups or a liter?

EXPLORE
Comparing Pounds and Kilograms

Jean wanted to figure out how kilograms compare with pounds. To do this, she put various weights on opposite sides of a balance scale.

 = 1 kg

 = 1 lb

1 What does this scale tell her?

2 What does this scale tell her?

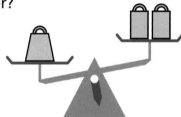

3 What does this scale tell her?

4 What does this scale tell her? Use a calculator to approximate the relation between pounds and kilograms.

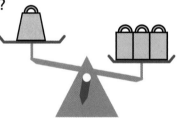

EXPLORE
Mystery Bags

Mr. Crepsi hid weights in boxes and bags. To figure out which weight is in a box and which weight is in a bag, he gave students these clues:

1 8 boxes balance a $\frac{1}{2}$-pound weight.

What weight could be in each box?

Why do you think so?

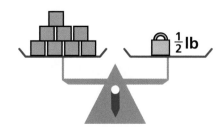

---

2 3 bags are heavier than 3 kilograms.

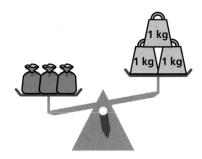

3 bags are a little lighter than 5 kilograms.

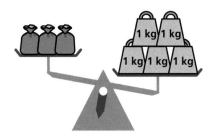

What weight could be in each bag?
Why do you think so?

REVIEW MODEL
Writing Equations and Inequalities

You can write equations and inequalities to represent the relation between weights on a scale.

If the scale is in balance . . .

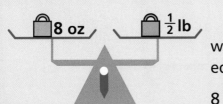

write an equation:

$8 \text{ oz} = \frac{1}{2} \text{ lb}$

If the scale is not in balance . . .

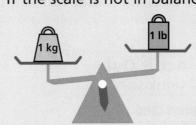

write an inequality:

$1 \text{ kg} > 1 \text{ lb}$

If you don't know the weight of an object on the scale, use a variable to represent the weight. You can use any letter or symbol for a variable, but x is the most common.

If the scale is in balance . . .

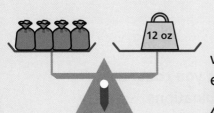

write an equation:

$4x = 12 \text{ oz}$

If the scale is not in balance . . .

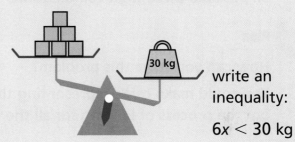

write an inequality:

$6x < 30 \text{ kg}$

✔ Check for Understanding

Write an equation or inequality to represent the picture.

❶

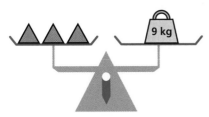

❷

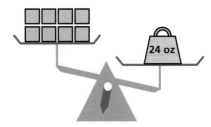

❸

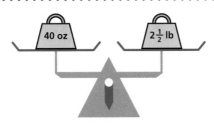

❹

REVIEW MODEL
Problem Solving Strategy
Act It Out

Gina has forgotten her three-digit locker combination. She remembers that the first digit is 5, the second digit is odd, and the third digit is either 7 or 8. How can she find all the possible locker combinations?

Strategy: Act it Out

Read to Understand

What do you know from reading the problem?

The first digit of Gina's three-digit locker combination is 5, the second digit is odd, and the third digit is either 7 or 8.

What do you need to find out?

all possible three-digit combinations

Plan

How can you solve this problem?

You could make cards representing the digits. Then you could act out the process of looking for all the possible combinations.

Solve

How can you *act it out* to solve the problem?

Make cards like these:

first   second   third

| 5 | | 1 | 3 | 5 | 7 | 9 | | 7 | 8 |

Then arrange them to make all the combinations of digits you can find: 517, 518, 537, 538, 557, 558, 577, 578, 597, 598. There are ten possible combinations that Gina must try.

Check

Look back at the problem. Did you answer the questions that were asked? Does the answer make sense?

The answer makes sense because there is 1 possible first digit, 5 possible second digits, and 2 possible third digits. I know from Chapter 10 that I can use multiplication to find numbers of attributes, and $1 \times 5 \times 2 = 10$.

Problem Solving Practice

Problem Solving Strategies

✔ **Act It Out**
✔ Draw a Picture
✔ Guess and Check
✔ Look for a Pattern
✔ Make a Graph
✔ Make a Model
✔ Make an Organized List
✔ Make a Table
✔ Solve a Simpler Problem
✔ Use Logical Reasoning
✔ Work Backward
✔ Write an Equation

Use the strategy *act it out* to solve.

❶ Six houses were arranged in a hexagon shape. One person lived in each house. One day, each person visited the house of every neighbor except the neighbors on either side of his or her house. How many house visits were made?

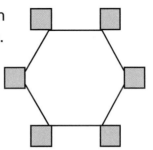

❷ In a word game, Beth drew the letters O, P, S, and T. She had to make a 4-letter word from the letters. How many different 4-letter combinations can she make from the letters?

Mixed Strategy Practice

Use any strategy to solve. Explain.

❸ From April 1 to May 1, the price of tomatoes doubled. From May 1 to June 1 it dropped $1, to $3 per pound. What was the price of tomatoes on April 1?

❹ On a balance scale, 6 quarters balance with 3 half dollars. Five dimes balance with 1 half dollar. How many dimes will balance with 2 quarters?

❺ A sofa is manufactured in 3 different styles, 3 different colors, and 2 different fabrics. How many style-color-fabric combinations does a buyer have to choose from?

❻ Toni rented a car for two days for $80. The charge the first day was $10 more than the second day. What was the charge the first day?

❼ Ben has 51 baseball cards and Jeff has 15 baseball cards. At the first Card Club meeting and every meeting thereafter, Ben sold 6 cards to Jeff. After which meeting did the two have equal numbers of cards?

❽ Ira bought three steaks, all priced the same, two loaves of bread, each costing $3, and a melon costing $2. The total cost of the items was $26. How much did each steak cost?

Chapter 15 Vocabulary

Choose the best vocabulary term from Word List A for each sentence.

1 Numbers that are easy to compute mentally are ___?___ numbers.

2 The number of square units needed to cover a surface is the ___?___ of the surface.

3 The distance around a figure is the ___?___ of the figure.

4 A metric unit for measuring capacity is the ___?___.

5 A customary unit for measuring weight is the ___?___.

6 A number sentence that shows that two quantities are equal is called a(n) ___?___.

7 The ___?___ is the measure of the amount of space a solid figure occupies.

8 The amount of matter in an object is its ___?___.

9 The ___?___ of an object tells how heavy it is.

Word List A

area
capacity
compatible
equation
inequality
kilogram
liter
mass
perimeter
quart
pound
round
scale
volume
weight

Complete each analogy using the best term from Word List B.

10 Quart is to ___?___ as kilogram is to mass.

11 Ruler is to inch as ___?___ is to pound.

Word List B

capacity
scale
inequality

Talk Math

Discuss with a partner what you have learned about estimation. Use the vocabulary terms *compatible* and *round*.

12 Ken's living room is a rectangle. How can you estimate its perimeter and area?

13 How can you use a liter to estimate a capacity in quarts?

14 How can you use a kilogram to estimate a weight in pounds?

Word Web

15 Create a word web for the word *round*.

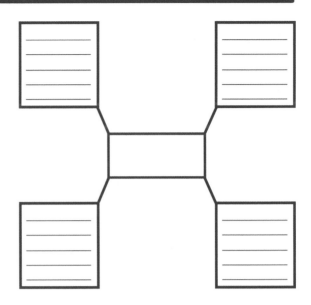

Word Line

16 Create a word line using the terms *cup, gallon, liter, milliliter,* and *quart.* Use what you know and what you have learned about estimation and measures of capacity.

Words:

Sequence:

What's in a Word?

SCALE This word has several different meanings. A *scale* is used on diagrams, such as maps and floor plans. It shows the relationship between the actual distance and the distance on the diagram. On a bar graph or line graph, a *scale* is a set of numbers placed at fixed distances to help label the graph. A balance *scale* is used to compare two weights. *Scales* are also part of the skin of a fish or reptile. A musical *scale* is a set of notes that go in order by pitch. A climber *scales* a mountain or cliff.

GAME

The Closest Estimate: Weight

Game Purpose
To practice estimating weight

Materials
- classroom objects (various)
- scale (that measures in grams/kilograms/ounces/pounds)
- clock

How To Play The Game

1 This is a game for 3 to 4 players. The goal is to look at various objects and estimate their weights. You score 1 point for each estimate that is the closest.

2 Choose several objects from your classroom. The objects must be able to be weighed on the scale. As a group, you may set a time limit, such as 30 seconds or 1 minute, for making each estimate. But a time limit is not necessary.

3 Display an object.
- Estimate the weight of the object in grams, ounces, pounds, or kilograms.
- Record your estimate on a sheet of paper.

4 Weigh the object on the scale. The player with the closest estimate gets 1 point.

5 Repeat steps 3 and 4 with the rest of the objects.

6 After you have used all the objects, add up your points. The player with the most points wins.

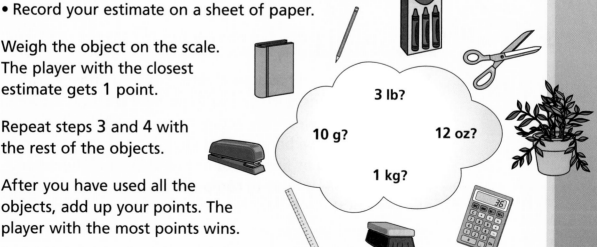

3 lb?

10 g?   12 oz?

1 kg?

GAME

Weight Match

Game Purpose
To practice applying the relationship between pounds and kilograms

Materials
• Activity Masters 155–156   • scissors

How To Play The Game

1 This is a game for 2 to 3 players. The object is to match pounds and kilograms. Remember, 1 kilogram is about 2.2 pounds.

2 Cut out all of the weight cards. Mix them up. Choose one player to deal all the cards to all players in the group.

• If you hold cards that name matching weights, place them face up on the table in front of you.

• Everyone should verify that the cards show approximately the same weights.

• If you made an incorrect match, take back your cards.

A Correct Match

| 10 kg | 22 lbs |

Not a Match

| 3 kg | 55 lbs |

3 After all correct matches have been made, the player to the left of the dealer picks a card from another player's hand.

• If the card matches a card already in the player's hand, he or she places the matching pair face up on the table.

• Everyone should verify the match.

• If the match is correct, the player chooses again. The same player continues to choose until he or she cannot make a match. Then it is the next player's turn.

4 Play until all cards have been matched and placed face up. The player with the most matches is the winner.

CHALLENGE

Each of the scales shown is unbalanced. What weight should be added to balance each scale?

1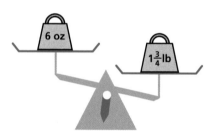

2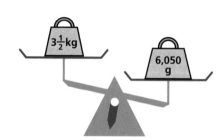

3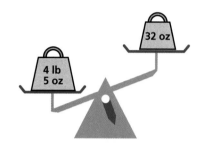

4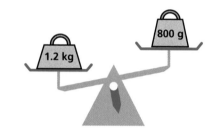

5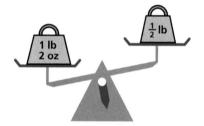

6

7

8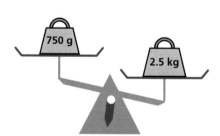

9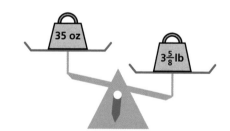

10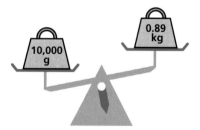

Table of Measures

METRIC | CUSTOMARY

LENGTH

METRIC	CUSTOMARY
1 centimeter (cm) = 10 millimeters (mm)	1 foot (ft) = 12 inches (in.)
1 decimeter (dm) = 10 centimeters	1 yard (yd) = 3 feet, or 36 inches
1 meter (m) = 100 centimeters (cm)	1 mile (mi) = 1,760 yards, or 5,280 feet
1 kilometer (km) = 1,000 meters	

CAPACITY

METRIC	CUSTOMARY
1 liter (L) = 1,000 milliliters (mL)	1 tablespoon (tbsp) = 3 teaspoons (tsp)
	1 cup (c) = 8 fluid ounces (fl oz)
	1 pint (pt) = 2 cups
	1 quart (qt) = 2 pints
	1 gallon (gal) = 4 quarts

MASS/WEIGHT

METRIC	CUSTOMARY
1 gram (g) = 1,000 milligrams (mg)	1 pound (lb) = 16 ounces (oz)
1 kilogram (kg) = 1,000 grams	1 ton (T) = 2,000 pounds

METRIC-CUSTOMARY COMPARISONS

Length: 1 meter is a little more than 1 yard (1 meter is about 1.09 yards)

Capacity: 1 liter is a little more than 1 quart (1 liter is about 1.06 quarts)

Mass/Weight: 1 kilogram is about 2.2 pounds

TIME

1 minute (min) =	60 seconds (sec)
1 hour (hr) =	60 minutes
1 day =	24 hours
1 week (wk) =	7 days
1 year (yr) =	12 months (mo), or about 52 weeks
1 year =	365 days
1 leap year =	366 days

MONEY

1 penny =	1 cent (¢)
1 nickel =	5 cents
1 dime =	10 cents
1 quarter =	25 cents
1 half dollar =	50 cents
1 dollar ($) =	100 cents

SYMBOLS

$<$	is less than	°	degree	$^{-}8$	negative 8
$>$	is greater than	°F	degrees Fahrenheit	(2,3)	ordered pair (x,y)
$=$	is equal to	°C	degrees Celsius	%	percent
$\neq$	is not equal to	$^{+}8$	positive 8		

FORMULAS

Perimeter of polygon = sum of length of sides	Area of rectangle $\quad A = l \times w$
Perimeter of rectangle $P = (2 \times l) + (2 \times w)$	Volume of rectangular
$= 2 \times (l + w)$	prism $\quad V = l \times w \times h$
Perimeter of square $P = 4 \times s$	

A

acute angle [ə•kyōōt′ ang′gəl] An angle that is smaller than a right angle

Example:

acute triangle [ə•kyōōt′ tri′•ang′gəl] A triangle with three acute angles

Example:

add [ad] To join two or more groups

Example:

3 + 2 = 5

addend [a′dend] A number that is added to another in an addition problem

Example: 2 + 4 = 6 ;
     2 and 4 are addends.

algebra [al′•jə•brə] Mathematics in which letters and symbols are used to represent numbers

angle [ang′gəl] A figure formed by two line segments or rays that share the same endpoint

Example:

area [âr′ē•ə] The number of square units needed to cover a surface

Example:

area = 9 square units

array [ə•rā′] An arrangement of objects in rows and columns

attribute [ə•trib′•yüt] A quality or feature of someone or something

axis (plural:axes) [ak′sis] The horizontal or vertical number line used in a coordinate plane; the line at the side or bottom of a graph

Example:

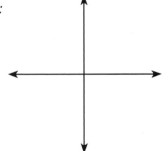

Glossary

bar graph [bär graf] A graph that uses bars to show data

base [bās] A number used as a repeated factor

Example: $8^3 = 8 \times 8 \times 8$. The base is 8.

base-seven [bās sev′•ən] A place value system in which the greatest single-digit number is 6

base-ten [bās ten] see base-ten system

base-ten system [bās ten sis′•təm] A place value system in which numbers are expressed using the numerals 0 to 9 and successive powers of 10

capacity [kə•pa′sə•tē] The amount a container can hold when filled

centimeter (cm) [sən′tə•mē•tər] A metric unit for measuring length or distance
100 centimeters = 1 meter

Example:

1 centimeter

certain [sər′tən] An event is certain if it will always happen

chart [chärt] Any display of data

column [ko•ləm] A vertical line in an array

Example:

↓ column

combine [kəm•bīn′] To put together

comma [kom′ə] The symbol used in large numbers to separate the hundreds from the thousands, the thousands from the millions, and so on

Example:

125,452,300

Commas

commutative property [kə•myü′•tə•tiv prop′•ər•tē] The property that states that when the order of addends or factors is changed, the sum or product is the same

Example: $9 + 4 = 4 + 9$.
$6 \times 3 = 3 \times 6$

compare [kəm•pār′] To describe whether numbers are equal to, less than, or greater than each other

compatible numbers [kəm•pa′tə•bəl num′bərz] Numbers that are easy to compute mentally

Example: Estimate $4{,}126 \div 8$.
  Think: 40 and 8 are compatible numbers.
  $4{,}126 \div 8$
    ↓   ↓
  $4{,}000 \div 8 = 500$
  So, $4{,}126 \div 8$ is about 500.

congruent [kən•grōō′ənt] Having the same size and shape

Example:

coordinate plane [kō•ôr′də•nət plān] A plane formed by two intersecting and perpendicular number lines called axes

Example:

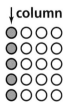

coordinates [kō•ôr′də•nāts] The numbers in an ordered pair

Example:

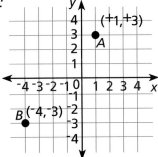

The coordinates of *A* are (1, 3).
The coordinates of *B* are (‾4, ‾3).

cubic [kyü′•bik] Relating to a cube

cup (c) [kup] A customary unit used to measure capacity

Example: 8 ounces = 1 cup

data [dā′tə] Information collected about people or things

decimal point [des′•ə•məl point] A symbol used to separate dollars from cents in money, and the ones place from the tenths place in decimal numbers

decimal portion [des′•ə•məl pôr′•shən] Digits to the right of a decimal point

Example: 3.**76**

decimal sums [des′•ə•məl sums] The result of adding decimal numbers

degree (°) [di•grē′] The unit used for measuring temperatures

denominator [di•nă′mə•nā•tər] The number below the bar in a fraction that tells how many equal parts are in the whole

Example: $\frac{3}{4}$ ← denominator

diagonal [di•ag′•ə•nəl] A line that connects two opposite corners of a figure

diagram [di′•ə•gram] A drawing that can be used to represent a situation

digit [di′•jət] Any one of the ten symbols 0, 1, 2, 3, 4, 5, 6, 7, 8, 9 used to write numbers

distance [dis′•təns] A measure of the length between two points

dimension [də•men′shən] A measure in one direction

distributive property [di•stri′byə•tiv prä′pər•tē] The property that states that multiplying a sum by a number is the same as multiplying each addend by the number and then adding the products

Example: 5 × (10 + 6) = (5 × 10) + (5 × 6)

divide [də•vīd′] To separate into equal groups

Example:

$$10 \div 5 = 2$$

divided by [də•vi•did bi] The term used to show the operation of division is to be used on a variable

dividend [di′və•dend] The number that is to be divided in a division problem

Example: 36 ÷ 6; 6)‾36; The dividend is 36.

division [də•vi′zhən] The process of sharing a number of items to find how many groups can be made or how many items will be in each group; the opposite operation of multiplication

divisor [də•vi′zər] The number that divides the dividend

Example: 15 ÷ 3; 3)‾15; The divisor is 3.

dollar notation [dol′•ər nō•tā′•shən] An application of the decimal system where places have the same value as in the decimal system, although they are read differently

Example: $4.25
        four dollars and twenty-five cents

dot [dot] A symbol used to represent multiplication

edge [ej] The line segment where two or more faces of a solid figure meet

Example:

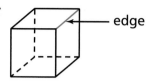 ← edge

eighth [ātth] The term to describe each of eight fractional parts

Example:

endpoint [end′•point] The point at the end of a line segment

Example:

endpoint

equal (=) [ē′•kwəl] A symbol used to show that two amounts have the same value

Example: 384 = 384

equation [i•kwā′zhən] A number sentence which shows that two quantities are equal

Example: 4 + 5 = 9

equilateral triangle [ē•kwə•la′tə•rəl trī′ang•əl] A triangle with 3 equal, or congruent, sides

Example:

6 cm 6 cm
6 cm

equivalent [ē-•kwiv′ə•lənt] Having the same value or naming the same amount

estimate [es′tə•māt] *verb* To find an answer that is close to the exact amount

estimate [es′tə•mət] *noun* A number close to an exact amount

face [fās] A polygon that is a flat surface of a solid figure

Example:

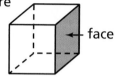 ← face

fact family [fakt fam′ə•lē] A set of related multiplication and division, or addition and subtraction, equations

Examples: 7 × 8 = 56; 8 × 7 = 56
56 ÷ 7 = 8; 56 ÷ 8 = 7

factor [fak′tər] A number multiplied by another number to find a product

factor pairs [fak′tər pārs] Factors that are paired within a fact family

fifth [fifth] The term to describe each of five fractional parts

Example:

flipping [fli′•ping] Moving a figure to a new position by flipping the figure over a line

Example:

foot (ft) [fŏŏt] A customary unit used for measuring length or distance

fourth [fôrth] The term to describe each of four fractional parts

Example:

fraction [frak′shən] A number that names a part of a whole or part of a group

function [fungk′•shən] A relationship between two quantities in which one quantity depends on the other

gallon (gal) [ga′lən] A customary unit for measuring capacity

Example: 4 quarts = 1 gallon

greater than (>) [grā′tər than] A symbol used to compare two quantities, with the greater quantities given first

Example: 6 > 4

greatest [grā′tist] The largest of something

grid [grid] Evenly divided and equally spaced squares on a figure or flat surface

height [hīt] The length of a perpendicular from the base to the top of a plane figure or solid figure

Example:

hexagon [hek′sə•gän] A polygon with six sides

Examples:

horizontal line [hôr′ə•zon′təl līn] A line drawn in a left-right direction

Examples:

0 1 2 3 4 5 6 7 8
horizontal

how many [hou men′ē] What the top number of a fraction shows

hundredth [hən′drədth] One of one hundred equal parts

Example:

impossible [im•pä′sə•bəl] Never able to happen

inch (in.) [inch] A customary unit used for measuring length or distance

Example:

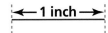

inequality [in•i•kwol′ə•tē] A mathematical sentence that shows two expressions do not represent the same quantity

Example: 4 < 9 − 3

intersecting lines [in•tər•sek′ting linz] Lines that cross each other at exactly one point

Example:

inverse operations [in′vərs ä•pə•rā′shənz] Operations that undo each other. Addition and subtraction are inverse operations. Multiplication and division are inverse operations.

Example: 5 + 4 = 9, so 9 − 4 = 5
3 × 4 = 12, so 12 ÷ 4 = 3

isosceles triangle [ī•sä′sə•lēz trī′ang•əl] A triangle with two equal, or congruent sides

Example:

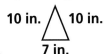

kilogram (kg) [ki′lə•gram] A metric unit for measuring mass

Example: 1 kilogram = 1,000 grams

least [lēst] The smallest of something

left [left] A direction found by referring to the left side of the body

leftover [left′•ō•vər] The extra numbers that cannot be divided evenly in a division problem

length [lenkth] The measure of a side of a figure

less than (<) [les than] A symbol used to compare two numbers, with the lesser number given first

Example: 3 < 7

likely [lik′lē] Having a greater than even chance of happening

line [lin] A straight path of points in a plane that continues without end in both directions with no endpoints

Example:
S   T

line of symmetry [lin ov sim′•ə•trē] A line that separates a figure into two congruent parts

Example:

line segment [lin seg′mənt] A part of a line that includes two points called endpoints and all the points between them

Example:
A   B

liter (L) [lēt′ər] A metric unit for measuring capacity

Example: 1 lilter = 1,000 millilters

lower [lou′ər] A location in reference to being below something else

mass [mas] The amount of matter in an object

median [mē′dē•ən] The middle number in an ordered set of data

meter (m) [mē′tər] A metric unit for measuring length or distance

Example: 100 centimeters = 1 meter

meter stick [mē′tər stik] A tool used to measure length in centimeters and meters

metric system [met′•rik sis′•təm] A measurement system that measures length in millimeters, centimeters, meters, and kilometers; capacity in liters and milliliters; mass in grams and kilograms; and temperature in degrees Celsius

middle [mid′•əl] A place in the center

milliliter (mL) [mi′lə•lē•tər] A metric unit for measuring capacity

Example: 1,000 milliliters = 1 liter

minus [mi′•nəs] A sign indicating subtraction

missing factor [mis′•ing fak′•tər] Unknown factors in a number sentence

Example: 6 × ＿＿ = 18
18 ÷ 6 = ＿＿

The missing factor is 3

mode [mōd] The number(s) or items(s) that occur most often in a set of data

multi-digit number [mul′•ti dij′•it num′•bər] A number that has more than one digit

multiple [mul′tə•pəl] The product of a given whole number and another whole number

multiplication [mul•tə•plə•kā ′shən] A process to find the total number of items in equal-sized groups, or to find the total number of items in a given number of groups when each group contains the same number of items; multiplication is the inverse of division

multiply [mul′tə•plī] To find the total number of items in equal-sized groups, or to find the total number of items in a given number of groups with each group contains the same number of items

Example:

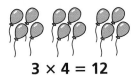

3 × 4 = 12

negative [ne′gə•tiv] All the numbers to the left of zero on the number line; negative numbers are less than zero

negative number [neg′•ə•tiv num′•bər] Any number less than zero

Example:

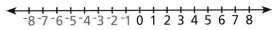

The red numbers are negative numbers.

net [net] A two-dimensional pattern that can be folded to make a three-dimensional figure

Example:

ninth [ninth] The term to describe each of nine fractional parts

Example:

non-decimal portion [non′ des′•ə•məl pôr′•shən] The portion of a number that is to the left of a decimal

Example: 53.76

numerator [noo′mə•rā•tər] The number above the bar in a fraction that tells how many equal parts of the whole are being considered

Example: $\frac{2}{3}$ ← numerator

obtuse angle [äb•toos′ ang′əl] An angle that is larger than a right angle but smaller than a straight angle

Example:

obtuse triangle [äb•toos′ tri′ang•əl] A triangle with one obtuse angle

Example:

operations [op•ə•rā′•shəns] Addition, subtraction, multiplication, and division

Example: operation signs: +, −, ×, ÷

order of operations [ôr′dər ov op•ə•rā′•shəns] Rules for performing operations in mathematical phrases with more than one operation

ordered pair [ôr′dərd pâr] A pair of numbers used to locate a point on a coordinate grid. The first number tells how far to move horizontally, and the second number tells how far to move vertically

origin [ôr′ə•jən] The point where the the x-axis and the y-axis in the coordinate plane intersect, (0,0)

outcome [out′kum] A possible result of an experiment

Glossary

packing [pa′•king] To exchange amounts of equal value to rename a number

parallel lines [par′•ə•lel linz] Lines in the same plane that never intersect and are always the same distance apart

Example:

parallelogram [par•ə•lel′ə•gram] A quadrilateral whose opposite sides are parallel and equal, or congruent

Example:

parentheses [pə•ren′thə•sēz] The symbols used to show which operation or operations in an expression should be done first

partial product [pär′•shəl prä′dəkt] A method of multiplying in which ones, tens, hundreds, and so on, are multiplied separately and then the products are added together

perimeter [pə•ri′mə•tər] The distance around a figure

perpendicular lines [pər•pən•di′kyə•lər linz] Two lines that intersect to form four right angles

Example:

pint (pt) [pīnt] A customary unit for measuring capacity

Example: 2 cups = 1 pint

place [plās] The location of digit in a number

place value [plās val′yoo] Place value determines the value of a digit in a number, based on the location of the digit

point [point] an exact location in space

polyhedra [pol•ē•hē•dra] Plural form of polyhedron

polyhedron [pol•ē•hē•drən] A solid figure with flat faces that are polygons

Examples:

positive numbers [pä′zə•tiv num′bərz] All the numbers to the right of zero on the number line; positive numbers are greater than 0

pound (lb) [pound] A customary unit for measuring weight

Example: 16 ounces = 1 pound

precision [pri•sizh′•ən] property of measurement related to the unit of measure used; the smaller the unit of measure used, the more precise the measurement is.

Example:

To the nearest inch, the crayon's length is 4 inches. A more **precise** measurement is $3\frac{15}{16}$ inches.

prism [priz′əm] Solid figure that has two congruent, polygon-shaped bases, and faces that are rectangles

Examples:

**rectangular   triangular
prism   prism**

probability [prä•bə•bil′ə•tē] The likelihood that an event will happen

product [prä′dəkt] The answer to a multiplication problem

pyramid [pir′ə•mid] A solid figure with a polygon base and triangular sides that meet at a single point

Example:

quadrilateral [kwä•drə•la′tə•rəl] A polygon with four sides

quart (qt) [kwôrt] A customary unit for measuring capacity *Example:* 2 pints = 1 quart

quotient [kwō′shənt] The number, not including the remainder, that results from dividing

Example: 8 ÷ 4 = 2; 2 is the quotient.

range [rānj] The distribution of data

reasonable [rē′•zə•nə•bəl] Sensible and logical

rectangle [rek′tang•əl] A parallelogram with opposite sides that are equal, or congruent, and with four right angles

Example:

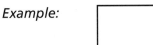

rectangular prism [rek•tang′gyə•lər pri′zəm] A solid figure in which all six faces are rectangles

Example:

reflecting [ri•flek′•ting] Moving a figure to a new position by flipping it over a line

Example:

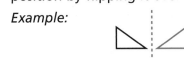

reflection (flip) [rē•flek′shən] A movement of a figure to a new position by flipping the figure over a line

Example:

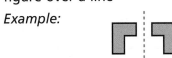

remainder [ri•mān′dər] The amount left over when a number cannot be divided equally

remaining [ri•mā•′ning] When there is a number left over that can not be divided equally

repacking [ri•pa′•king] To exchange amounts of equal value to rename a number

Example: 23 = 2 tens 3 ones
or 1 ten 13 ones

rhombus [räm′bəs] A parallelogram with four equal, or congruent sides

Example:

right [rīt] A direction is found by referring to the right side of the body

right angle [rīt ang′əl] An angle that forms a square corner

Example:

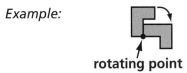

right triangle [rīt tri′ang′•əl] A triangle with one right angle

Example:

rotating [rō•tā•ting] Moving a figure to a new position by turning the figure around a point

Example:

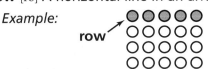

rotating point

round [round] To replace a number with another number that tells about how many or how much

row [rō] A horizontal line in an array

Example:

row

Glossary

S

scale [skāl] A series of numbers placed at fixed distances on a graph to help label the graph

scalene triangle [skā′lēn trī′ang•əl] A triangle with no equal, or congruent, sides

Example:

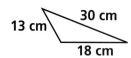

seventh [sev′•ənth] The term to describe each of seven fractional parts

Example:

side [sīd] A straight line that makes up part of a figure

sixth [siksth] The term to describe each of six fractional parts

Example:

sliding [slīd•ing] See *translating*

square [skwâr] A parallelogram with 4 equal, or congruent, sides and 4 right angles

Example:

square number [skwâr num′bər] The product of a number and itself

Example: $4^2 = 16$; 16 is a square number.

square unit [skwâr yoo′nət] A unit of area with dimensions of 1 unit × 1 unit

sum [sum] The answer to an addition problem

symbol [sim′•bəl] Something that represents something else

symmetric [si•met′•rik] When a figure has a line of symmetry

symmetry [sim′ə•trē] When one half of a figure looks like the mirror image of the other half

Example:

T

table [tā′•bəl] A tool to organize data that consists of columns and rows

tenth [tenth] One of ten equal parts

Example:

tenths [tenths] A decimal or fraction that names 1 part of 10 equal parts

Example:

$\frac{1}{10}$ or 0.1

ton (T) [tun] A customary unit for measuring weight

Example: 2,000 pounds = 1 ton

total [tō′•təl] The final amount found when adding or multiplying

total area [tō′•təl ār′•ē•ə] The sum of the areas of all the faces, or surfaces, of a solid figure

translating [tra′ns•lā•ting] Moving a figure to a new position along a straight line

Example:

trapezoid [tra′pə•zoid] A quadrilateral with exactly one pair of parallel sides

Example:

triangle [trī′ang•əl] A polygon with three sides

Example:

turning [tûrn] A movement of a figure to a new position by rotating the figure around a point

Example:

unit [yü′•nit] A standard quantity used in measurement

unlikely [un•li′klē] Having a less than even chance of happening

unpacking [un•pa′•king] To exchange amounts of equal value to rename a number

upper [up′•ər] A location above something else

variable [vâr′ē•ə•bəl] A letter or symbol that stands for a number or numbers

vertex [vûr′teks] The point at which two rays of an angle or two or more sides meet in a plane figure, or where three or more edges meet in a solid figure; the top point of a cone

Example:

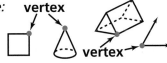

vertical format [vûr′•tə•kəl fôr′•mat] A method to show addition where the addends are in the top portion, and the sum is at the bottom

vertical line [vûr′•tə•kəl līn] A line drawn in an up-down direction

Example:

vertices [vûr′•tə•sēz] Plural of vertex

volume [väl′yəm] The measure of the amount of space a solid figure occupies

weight [wāt] How heavy an object is

what kind [hwot kīnd] What the bottom part of a fraction shows

whole number [hōl num′bər] One of the numbers 0, 1, 2, 3, 4 . . . ; the set of whole numbers goes on without end

width [witth] A measurement of a figure from one side to another

x, y, z [eks wī zē] The letters commonly used in algebraic expressions to represent missing variables

yard (yd) [yärd] A customary unit for measuring length or distance

Example: 3 feet = 1 yard

zero [zē•rō] The number (0) between the set of all negative numbers and the set of all positive numbers

Example:

Index

A

Act It Out, 134–135, 152–153, 184–185, 250–251

Acute triangle, 59

Addition
decimals, 132
different units, 144
Eraser Store shipment orders, 41

Algebraic thinking
applying squaring pattern, 231
bags and counters, 227
Number Puzzle Mystery, 226
product near square numbers, 230
shorthand notation, 228
Student Letter, 223

Angles
Student Letter, 55
in triangles, 58–59

Area
compare, 74
compare to perimeter, 79
faces of three-dimensional figures, 179
finding, 244
rectangle, 179
for strange figure, 76
Student Letter, 71
triangles, 77
using transformations to find, 75

Area model
for division, 210

Arrays
adding array sections for multiplication, 20
arrange twenty-four tiles, 27
combining multiplication facts, 22
to model multiplication, 91–92
for multiplication shortcuts, 23
rows and columns in (for multiplication), 25–27
separating arrays in different ways for multiplication, 21

splitting larger for multi-digit multiplication, 92

B

Balance scale, 249

Bar graphs
making, 167

Base-ten blocks
adding decimals, 132
packaging multiple identical shipments, 42
representing decimals, 131
subtracting decimals, 133

C

Capacity
comparing units of, 246
liters compared to gallons, 245

Centimeters
measuring, 148
reading ruler, 149

Certain event, 162

Challenge, 16, 34, 54, 70, 86, 102, 122, 140, 158, 174, 190, 206, 222, 238, 256

Classify
parallelograms, 61

Compare
area, 74, 79
decimals, 129–130
fractions, 111–112, 129–130
liters to gallons, 245
perimeter, 79
units of capacity, 246

Cone
recognizing, 178

Congruent figures, 74

Conversions
adding different units, 144
inches and feet, 147

Index

Photo Credits

CHAPTER 1: 2 (c) Corel; 2 (bg) Ralph A. Clevenger/CORBIS; 3 (bl) Don Smetzer/Photo Edit; (r) Getty Images

CHAPTER 2: 18 (bg) AP Photo/Chris Pizzello; 19 (cr) Masterfile

CHAPTER 3: 36 (bg) Ambient Images/Alamy; (r) Photodisc; 37 (r) Getty Images

CHAPTER 4: 56 (cl) E & S Ginsberg/Alamy; (cr) Leslie Garland Picture Library/Alamy; (bg) Jeff Greenberg/PhotoEdit; 57 (tr) Jeremy Woodhouse/Masterfile

CHAPTER 5: 72 (bg) Carol & Mike Werner/Age Fotostock; 73 (tr) Getty Images

CHAPTER 6: 88 (bg) Pictorial Press Ltd/Alamy; (t) Alamy; (tc) Getty Images; (bc) Alamy; (b) Jupiter Images; 89 (bl) Underwood & Underwood/CORBIS

CHAPTER 7: 104 (bg) CORBIS; (tr) Wesley Bocxe/Getty Images; (bl) CORBIS; 105 (tr) SuperStock

CHAPTER 8: 124 (bg) Handke-Neu/zefa/CORBIS; (tr) AP Photo/Akron Beacon Journal, Ken Love; 125 (tr) AP Photo/Akron Beacon Journal, Ken Love

CHAPTER 9: 142 (cr) Mike Powell/Getty Images; (tr) Getty Images; (tr) Nick Daly/Getty Images; (cr) Alamy; (br) Getty Images; (bl) Barbara Peacock/Getty Images; 143 (cr) Bob Scott/Getty Images; (tr) Tracy Kahn/CORBIS

CHAPTER 10: 160 (br) Jeff Chandler/Shutterstock; (bl) Steven Vona/Shutterstock; (tc) Alamy; (tl) A. T. Willett/Alamy; (tr) CORBIS; (cl) CORBIS; (cr) Martyn F. Chillmaid, photographersdirect; (cr) Quayside Graphics, photographersdirect; 161 (r) Jeff Chandler/Shutterstock

CHAPTER 11: 176 (bg) Paul Burley Photography/Getty Images; (tr) Alamy; 177 (bg) Paul Burley Photography/Getty Images

CHAPTER 12: 192 (bg) Randy Lincks/Masterfile; (tr) Paul Barton/CORBIS; (br) CORBIS; 193 (tl) CORBIS

CHAPTER 13: 208 (bg) Bill Steele/Getty Images; (tr) Joe Bator/CORBIS; (br) CORBIS; 209 (cr) Walter Bibikow/JAI/CORBIS

CHAPTER 14: 224 (br) The Great Train Story, Museum of Science and Industry, Chicago, IL; (tr) The Great Train Story, Museum of Science and Industry, Chicago, IL; 225 (cr) The Great Train Story, Museum of Science and Industry, Chicago, IL; (br) Gerald S. Williams/NewsCom

CHAPTER 15: 240 (bg) isifa Image Service s.r.o./Alamy; (tr) Kim Taylor/Nature Picture Library; 241 (tr) Kim Taylor/Nature Picture Library; (cr) Alamy

Other photos used by permission of Houghton Mifflin Harcourt.